PDF Printing and Publishing

The next revolution after Gutenberg

Mattias Andersson
William Eisley
Amie Howard
Frank Romano
Mark Witkowski

Rochester Institute of Technology

Foreword by John Warnock, Chairman, Adobe Systems, Inc.
Afterword by Michael Jahn

A Publication of
Agfa Division, Bayer Corp.

Bookstore distribution by
Micro Publishing Press
Torrance, CA

PDF Printing and Publishing

The next revolution after Gutenberg

Mattias Andersson
William Eisley
Amie Howard
Frank Romano
Mark Witkowski

Micro Publishing Press
2340 Plaza Del Amo, Suite 100
Torrance, CA 90501
(310) 212-5802

First Printing: March, 1997

Printed in the United States of America

ISBN 0-941845-22-2

Intellectual Property

To retain some semblance of readability we omitted trademark information for all products mentioned. Here is the list:

Adobe, the Adobe logo, Acrobat, the Acrobat logo, Acrobat Catalog, Acrobat Capture, Acrobat Exchange, Acrobat Distiller, Acrobat Reader, Acrobat Search, Adobe Accurate Screens, Adobe Type Manager, Adobe Type Set, Adobe Illustrator, Aldus, ATM, the ATM logo, Display PostScript, PageMill, the PageMill logo, Photoshop, the Photoshop logo, PrintMill, Pixelburst, PageMaker, PostScript, and the PostScript logo are registered trademarks of Adobe Systems Incorporated.

Agfa, the Agfa rhombus, Agfa Balanced Screening, Agfa, Mainstream, AgfaType, AccuSet, Alliance, Alto, Arcus, Avantra, ChromaPost, Chromapress, ChromaWatch, ChromaWrite, Cobra, CristalRaster, DuoProof, FotoLook, FotoTune, Horizon, IntelliTrack, LUTGen, MultiStar, OptiSpot, PhotoWise, ProSlide, Python, QuickLink, SelectScan, SelectSet, Setprint, Star, Taipan and Viper are trademarks of Bayer Corporation or its affiliates, which may be registered in certain jurisdictions.

AppleTalk, EtherTalk, ColorSync, ImageWriter, LaserWriter, Mac, Macintosh, Macintosh Quadra and QuickTime are trademarks of Apple Computer, Inc. registered in the U.S. and other countries and AppleScript, Power Macintosh, PowerBook, QuickDraw, System 6, System 7 and TrueType are trademarks of Apple Computer, Inc.

Ethernet is a registered trademark of Xerox Corp.

Freehand is a trademark of Macromedia Corp.

HP, LaserJet and PCL are registered trademarks of Hewlett-Packard Company.

IBM and OS/2 are registered trademarks of International Business Machines Corporation.

Kodak is a registered trademark of Eastman Kodak Company.

Linotype, Hell, Optima, Helvetica, Palatino, Times, and Univers are registered trademarks and HQS Screening, LinoPress, LinoServer, Linotype Library, RT Screening, are trademarks of Linotype-Hell AG and/or its subsidiaries.

Microsoft and MS-DOS are registered trademarks and Windows, Windows 95 and Windows NT are trademarks of Microsoft Corporation.

Novell and NetWare are registered trademarks of Novell, Inc.

OpenWindows, Sun, SunOS, are trademarks of Sun Microsystems, Inc.

Post-It is a registered trademark of 3M.

Scitex is a registered trademark of Scitex Corp.

Solaris is a registered trademark of Sun Microsystems, Inc.

SPARCstation is a registered trademark of SPARC International, Inc., licensed exclusively to Sun Microsystems, Inc and is based upon an architecture developed by Sun Microsystems, Inc.

UNIX is a registered trademark in the U.S. and other countries, licensed exclusively through X/Open Company, Ltd.

QuarkXPress and QuarkXTension are registered trademarks of Quark, Inc.

All other company and brand and product names are trademarks, registered trademarks or service marks of their respective holders. And if we inadvertently missed anyone, any word with a capital letter is probably a trademark of somebody's.

ACKNOWLEDGMENTS

General

John Warnock, Dianne Eckloff, Eric Bean and Jennifer Polanski at Adobe Systems, Inc.

Peter Broderick, John Harrison, Paul Verwilt and Rick Littrell at Agfa.

The gifted Peter Miller who designed the cover and some of the illustrations.

Maureen Richards and everyone at United Lithograph.

The irrepressible Michael Jahn of 4Sight.

Larry Warter of Fuji Photo Film who contributed material and input on standards.

Mohan Kumar Dhandapani for being Mohan Kumar Dhandapani.

Daniel Wallin, ColorCraft AB.

Professor Frank Cost for his unique insights and great conversation.

RIT Campus Safety for checking on us during those 2am sessions.

Jim Cavuoto and Richard Romano at Micro Publishing Press.

The gang in the RIT Electronic Prepress and Publishing Laboratory, especially Chris Hahn and Peter Muir and all their "labbies."

Hal Gaffin and Bill Birkett of the RIT School of Printing for their support.

The people who hooked up our RIT ID and debit cards to the coffee and junk food machines.

GTS Graphics in City of Commerce, CA, who output the film for this book on an Agfa Avantra 44 imagesetter.

Personal

I would like to thank Amie, Bill, and Mark for their patience with switching the keybord setting back to US after I had left it on Swedish, and teaching me when to use *have* and *has*. Without the lectures from Frank Cost I would not have gotten the sparkling thought of how PDF can be used as the future of electronic publishing. — *Mattias Andersson*

Summing up three months of intense labor into three sentences is tough, but here goes . . . Thanks to: my mother for believing in me and giving me the chance, Phil & Jim for my sanity, and finally Frank Romano for the opportunity to work with Amie, Mark & Mattias. Working with such a diverse group of talent was a great learning experience.
— *William Eisley*

First, to Frank Romano for the opportunity. To Michael for getting us started, seeing us through, and finishing it off. To the Gang of Four, for being such good guys. And to my family . . . To Mindy, for your spirit and enthusiasm which have always been and inspiration. To Mom and Dad, my role models, my best friends, my heroes, . . . for all you are and all you do.
— *Amie Howard*

I would like to thank my parents, family and friends who's love and support have given me the values and drive to make me who I am today. To the other members of The Gang of Four, thanks for making this project so great. And to Frank Romano . . . thanks a million!
— *Mark Witkowski*

TABLE OF CONTENTS

FOREWORD

Adobe Systems is known for developing software that lets users easily create the most visually rich documents. One of the most complex challenges I've faced in 35 years in the software industry is devising technology for communicating these documents electronically, as well as on paper.

Adobe's groundbreaking PostScript technology—the basis for the desktop publishing revolution—inspired a fresh approach to the problem. Instead of attempting to electronically replicate documents from their original authoring applications, as earlier industry efforts had done, Adobe looked to the printing stage of the document creation process. Soon after the introduction of Adobe PostScript, practically every desktop computer on all major operating systems contained a PostScript driver for outputting documents to print. So why not convert documents to a new electronic format at the output stage, using the virtually universal Adobe PostScript language as the basis? Then, with cross-platform viewing software, anyone could easily access even the most visually rich content, no matter what application had been used to create it.

Portable Document Format (PDF) is the realization of Adobe's unique approach. PDF allows you to electronically communicate even the most visually dazzling document, free from the constraints of operating systems and applications, without sacrificing its look and feel.

Leading-edge printers, prepress service providers, and imaging companies recognized the enormous potential of PDF and soon began using it to streamline their workflows and cut costs. And today, PDF is poised to become a standard for communicating information on the Internet.

As the novelty of the World Wide Web fades, corporations, publishers, and designers want to take advantage of the Internet's potential to accomplish basic business goals, such as attracting customers, making information readily accessible, and enhancing productivity. More sophisticated users demand a more elegant method for delivering information on the Internet. The ease of use, universality, and unmatched visual quality of PDF position it with HTML as the ideal solution for communicating ideas on-line.

Meeting the challenges of printing and electronically communicating visually rich documents has been one of the most satisfying accomplishments of my career. Today, the vast potential of the Internet has brought Adobe— indeed, the entire business world—to a new crossroads. PDF has led Adobe to exciting new places we never expected to visit. And I am confident that exploring the possibilities of PDF will make the future just as exciting.

John Warnock
Chairman and Chief Executive Officer
Adobe Systems Incorporated

FIVEWORD

(it comes after a foreword)

Everything starts with an idea.

But then someone has to make it a reality.

In the Fall of 1996 I taught the graduate-level class called "Trends in the Graphic Arts." During that class I described how the new version of Adobe Acrobat (now called 3.0) was going to change the world of digital printing and publishing. During a visit by Richard Benson, dean of the Yale School of Art and Peter Broderick, of Agfa, I mentioned that a team of students and myself were working on a book on the subject.

Agfa said that they were developing new pre-press workflows that integrated the Acrobat PDF and were interested in sponsoring the work. One thing led to another and Jim Cavuoto at Micro Publishing Press agreed to publish the book and four students suddenly were about to become published authors. They are:

> Mattias Andersson
> William Eisley
> Amie Howard
> Mark Witkowski

They took Acrobat 3.0 apart and put it back together. The result is a book that tells you how to use 3.0 for high-end printing and publishing and describes the evolution and application of new workflows. They did all this while working towards their Masters of Science degrees at the same time.

They worked tirelessly to meet the deadlines and produce a work that would really matter. They travelled to conferences in Florida twice (during the winter?) and to Massachusetts (during the winter!).

Our goal in this book has been to explore the application of the Adobe Acrobat 3.0 PDF and especially its place in new workflows that automate the printing and publishing industries. We are truly appreciative of Agfa and their continuing support of industry education. This book is only one small part of their many publications and programs.

It has truly been a team effort and I am very proud to be one of the five authors who made this book a reality.

Frank Romano
Melbert B. Cary Jr. Distinguished Professor
of Graphic Arts
School of Printing Management & Sciences
Rochester Institute of Technology

CHAPTER

POST-GUTENBERG TO POSTSCRIPT

The title of this book was not created lightly. The Adobe Portable Document Format is the next revolution after Gutenberg.

Good old Johann Gutenberg did not invent printing. The term and the concept existed before he did and was practiced at the same time he lived. Playing cards and other materials were printed from carved blocks of wood.

Gutenberg assembled a system, from presses and ink to moveable type. The result was mechanical or automated writing, as one of his un-signed colophons stated. This became the mechanism for improved information dissemination, the growth of knowledge and the development of western civilization. Not bad for a goldsmith.

Gutenberg invented a method for communicating more information, in a more timely fashion to more people than ever before. And that's what the PDF does. With Version 3.0 it extends its franchise into high-end printing while maintaining its lead in document transmission and viewing.

Cave drawings, hieroglyphics, Gutenberg bibles, and glossy magazines are all information containers. Although the form of each container is radically different, the end purpose is the same—to share and distribute information and ideas.

Today, we call these information containers—documents. To have value, these documents and the information contained within them must be easily shared and distributed.

Until Gutenberg and his invention of movable type, documents were only available to the elite because they were so valuable. A book or bible might take years to be painstakingly hand copied by a monk or scribe. The ability to share documents with a large number of people was just not a possibility.

Movable type changed that. Mass production of books allowed for a wider spread of information. Similar to the automobile mass production revolution of the 1900s which made cars affordable to huge numbers of people, books were beginning to become a commodity, not a rarity. This revolution continues today. From movable type, to phototypesetting and imagesetting, to 16-page computer-to-plate signatures, the publishing/printing industry strives for faster and more effective ways of mass producing documents.

In the Beginning

As document creation evolved into computerized forms, document composition was primarily limited to proprietary Color Electronic Prepress Systems (CEPS). These systems, produced by companies such as Linotype-Hell and Scitex, were not only expensive but difficult to use. Another drawback to these proprietary systems was the difficulty or impossibility of cross platform file transfer.

The Revolution

March 21, 1985 marked the date when easy, economical digital publishing became a reality. On this day Apple, Aldus, Adobe, and Linotype unveiled a working typesetting system with an open architecture. It was based on the Macintosh Plus computer, which was one of the first personal computers with a Graphical User Interface, GUI. The output was made with either a laser printer, the Apple LaserWriter, or a high resolution imagesetter, Linotronic 300, from Linotype. Both output devices operated with a new Page Description Language (PDL), called PostScript from Adobe. The typesetting front end utilized software from Aldus PageMaker, which was a graphic-oriented page layout program operating on the Macintosh.

The strength and importance of this prepress system was that several graphic arts industry vendors worked together on an open-architecture system that would be available to everyone at a fraction of the price of a CEPS system. During the years after the introduction of the new system based on the PostScript page imaging model, more and more printer and imagesetter manufacturers implemented PostScript into their output systems.

Further developments in the prepress industry have produced devices for scanning, page assembly, and output which are compatible with the desktop publishing system based on PostScript. As a result of these combined efforts, digital workflows have been able to significantly speed up prepress production and related turnaround times.

Today, anyone with a computer can be a publisher. The publisher can choose from a wide range of applications, typefaces and output devices all speaking the same tongue, PostScript.

A Little About PostScript
The idea for PostScript began in 1976 as a Computer Assisted Design (CAD) language called Interpress at Xerox's Palo Alto Research Center. When Xerox abandoned the project, John Warnock and Chuck Geschke left and formed Adobe in 1981. Their first product was PostScript.

PostScript's power lies in the fact that it is a device-independent programming language. This means that the same PostScript file can be output on any device regardless of its resolution. As a programming language, PostScript can support any level of graphic complexity. Loop routines can be set to define extremely complex patterns and objects.

While looping capabilities are a boon, they can also be a bane.

Phototypesetters
Character-based typesetters on film or photo paper.

CRT phototypesetters
Character, line art and some photo using cathode ray tubes for higher speeds.

Laser phototypesetters
Character, line art and photo output via lasers.

Laser imagesetters
Character, line art and photo in color primarily to film — capstan or drum based.

Laser imposetters
Character, line art and photo in color for imposed flats of 4-up, 8-up and more pages.

Laser platesetters
Character, line art and photo in color for imposed polyester and aluminum plates.

Laser imaged on-press plates
Character, line art and photo in color for imposed plates in registration on press.

PostScript Interpreter
Parses and interprets PostScript codes and operators.

Display List
A list of all of the objects on a page.

Rasterizer
Builds the page from the list of objects in the Display List and creates a page bitmap for the output device.

PostScript files could contain loops that take two hours to process without ever placing a single mark on a page. Another boon/bane is PostScript's flexibility. Aside from syntax rules, the format of PostScript is very unstructured. There are an infinite number of ways to write code to perform the same task. Some of these ways are extremely efficient and others are not.

This relationship is best seen in the way some software applications generate "good, RIPable" PostScript data and other software generates "poor, problematic" PostScript data.

Due its unstructured nature, PostScript is an extremely page-dependent page description language. Page-dependence means that the entire file must be interpreted prior to imaging a single page. As a result, the individual pages described within a PostScript file cannot be easily extracted from that file. In other words, an object, like a circle, placed on the first page of a document, may not be described by the PostScript code until the end of the file. The unstructured nature of PostScript and its page dependence leads to a very unpredictable file format.

A RIP

In a sense, the RIP, or raster image processor, is really the PostScript programming language compiler. It interprets the file and "executes" its commands which are to draw objects on a page. A RIP is the essential element in any form of raster-based imaging which includes computer-to: paper, film, plate, cloth, plastic, metal and perhaps epidermis. The end result of ripping is a bitmap for the entire image that tells the output engine where to place dots.

The RIP performs three functions:
1. Interpretation of the page description language from the application program
2. Display list generation
3. Rasterizing (making the bitmap)

Almost every imaging device available today is a raster imager—using dots to build text, lines, photos, etc. Thus, every imager must, out of necessity, have a RIP, whether it is a lowly desktop printer or a giant computer-to-plate (CTP) system. And every RIP is just a little bit different. Many are based on Adobe's design, with some additional features, and some are legally derived from public information on the PostScript language. These have been called PostScript clones. Most of the small or home office market is dominated by Hewlett-Packard's PCL printer language, a PostScript wanna be.

When you send a document to a printer the RIP does its job and out come the page or pages. But today's digital workflow is much more complex and multiple rippings are often the norm. In a CTP workflow, the document might be ripped to a color printer for color proofing, ripped to an imposition proofer, ripped to a remote proofer, and finally ripped to the platesetter. In most cases this involves four different RIPs and four different imaging engines. And four chances for variation.

Over time, two paths to RIP development took place by:
- Adobe licensees
- Adobe clones

In both cases, the RIP includes a core set of functions based on a PostScript interpreter. From there developers have added increasing functionality. Here are some of them:
- More efficient graphics handling
- More efficient picture handling
- Halftone screening with different dot structures, angles, and algorithms
- Stochastic screening
- Trapping
- Imposition
- Statistics and other reports

RIP Evolution
The PostScript page description language was developed to communicate the appearance of text, graphical shapes, and images to raster-based output devices equipped with a PostScript interpreter. PostScript has become predominant in the computer printing world because of its device-independence. Device-independence means that the image (the page to print or display) is defined without any reference to specific device features (printer resolution, page size, etc.). A single page

description can be used on any PostScript-compatible printer from a 300 dpi laser printer to a 3,000+ dpi imagesetter or plate-setter. In our opinion, another reason for its success is that it supports high-end printing. Computer-to-plate and digital printing as we know them could not have developed without a standardized page description language.

Most applications that can print to a PostScript printer also let you "print" to a file. Printing to a file means that the application (or the computer running the application, with the help of a PostScript driver) converts the job data to PostScript commands and saves it as a file instead of transmitting the code to a printer. You can download the file to any PostScript printer to print the file. Downloading is different from printing in that no data conversion (from job data to PostScript) takes place, the file is merely sent to the printer. This allows you to directly send PostScript streams to printers, without opening any application program. Most computer platforms have a variety of PostScript downloaders available.

PostScript Printer Description Files
Each application usually creates and stores files in its own internal format, not PostScript. When you print a job, the application uses a PostScript driver to translate its data into PostScript. Depending on what computer or application you use, the printer driver could be installed as part of the application, or, more commonly, the printer driver is installed in the System folder for any application to use.

PostScript is device independent . . . to a point. When you print, you print to a specific printer that has very specific features such as certain resolutions, page sizes, minimum margins, choice of paper trays, etc. Although the PostScript driver can send the PostScript job to any printer, it can't specify a tabloid page for a printer that does not have a tabloid tray, for example. To access features specific to the printer, PostScript uses PPDs (PostScript Printer Description files) which are stored in the System folder.

Some printer-specific information that a PPD might include:
- Input paper trays
- Page size definitions

- Print areas for each page size
- Output paper trays
- Duplexing (double-sided printing)
- Default resolution
- Resolutions available
- Black and white or color output
- Halftone screening functions
- Default screen angles
- Screen frequency combinations
- Custom screening definition
- Default transfer functions
- Default font

QuarkXPress also uses another file to relate printer-specific information: a Printer Description File (PDF), which is not to be confused with the subject of this book, the Portable Document Format, also a PDF. (Silly, isn't it?) QuarkXPress uses data from both the PPD and PDF to generate PostScript for output.

At print time, you select the PostScript output device and select a PPD (and a PDF in QuarkXPress). If you later want to print the same job to a different printer, all you need to do is select a different printer with a different PPD.

PostScript Interpreters and RIPs
When the RIP receives the PostScript file for processing, it needs to convert that file to bitmap data. PostScript printers, whether 300 dpi laser printers or 3,000+ dpi platesetters, need a PostScript interpreter to translate the PostScript code into the bitmap data needed to print or image the page. Raster data prints a page as a pattern of tiny printer dots or spots. To place these dots, the RIP maps out the page as a grid of spot locations—this is called a bitmap. Any specific spot can be defined or located by its address based on x,y coordinates. To image a page, the output engine either images a spot or does not—zero or one, on or off. Data of this type is called binary, because only two values are used.

Bitmap data is what the output engine or recorder needs. But PostScript really describes pages not as a table of spots, but as a series of mathematically described shapes or objects. It takes a

PDF, PPD and PDF: What is what?

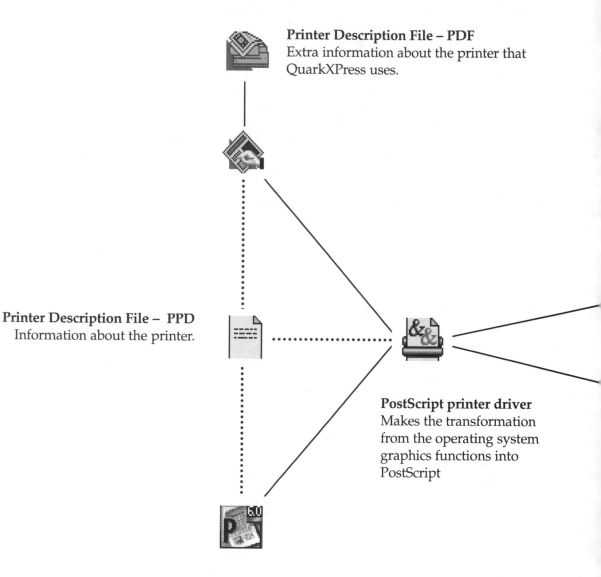

Printer Description File – PDF
Extra information about the printer that QuarkXPress uses.

Printer Description File – PPD
Information about the printer.

PostScript printer driver
Makes the transformation from the operating system graphics functions into PostScript

PostScript File
Includes the same information that would be sent to a PostScript printer

Acrobat Distiller
Application that interprets PostScript data and builds a Portable Document Format file

Portable Document Format – PDF
A device-independent document format

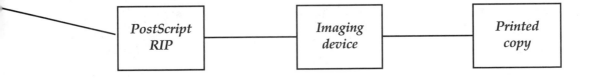

Dots and Spots and Pixels

Most imaging recorders today use a laser. The laser creates a SPOT whose size is based on the resolution of the recorder. This is the basic laser SPOT and its width is measured in micron—thousandths of an inch.

Over in the printing world pictures are reproduced on printing presses as patterns of halftone dots. These are clusters of black that fool the eye into perceiving a level of gray. Thus a DOT should refer to a halftone dot. But many of us use the terms dot and spot as though they were the same.

It takes a bunch, maybe 10, of the laser SPOTs to make a halftone DOT.

SPOTs are on or off, black or not there. PIXELS are generated by video monitors or some specialized recorders and they are SPOTs with varying levels of energy. A PIXEL can be 100% dark or at some percentage of gray. Thus Red, Green and Blue PIXELs can be combined at varying levels to display a picture.

Once again the term PIXEL is often used for SPOT or DOT. But now you know the difference.

lot less data to describe a page by its shape, size, and location than by listing the state (on or off) of each individual pixel in the image. The PostScript interpreter converts the PostScript code to a list of objects. Then it rasterizes the objects to create the bitmap for actual outputting. The resolution of the output device determines how many spots are needed to image a page.

PostScript Level 2

Since the introduction of PostScript in 1985, Adobe and other developers have created extensions to the PostScript language. Color extensions were added in 1988 to better support printing color images. PostScript Level 2 was announced in 1990, and it integrated the original PostScript with all previous language extensions, and added new features. Included in PostScript Level 2:

- **Color separation:** Lets a user send a full-color job, not already separated, to the PostScript Level 2 interpreter which converts the one-page color job into four files: one for each process color (cyan, magenta, yellow, and black).
- **Composite fonts:** Type 1 PostScript fonts can encode 256 distinct characters but a typical Japanese font has over 7,000 characters. The composite font technology included in PostScript Level 2 supports these larger fonts.
- **Data compression:** Network transmission is a large percentage of the actual processing time for a job. PostScript Level 2 supports several data compression schemes, such as LZW, JPEG, and RLE. Jobs sent over the network are sent in a compressed format, then decompressed by the PostScript interpreter. The amount of data transmitted is reduced, speeding up the network transmission portion of the job.

Hardware and Software RIPs

There are so-called hardware RIPs and software RIPs. The distinction is not always clear. Initially all RIPs were proprietary, with a CPU, disk, RIP software, and related hardware enclosed in a cabinet and attached to an imaging recorder. There was no monitor and no keyboard, although a keypad and LCD panel on the recorder did allow some level of interface. You connected your network to the RIP and away you went. Then someone decided that they could sell you the RIP software and you could install it in your own computer. Usually they supplied a special computer board and cable to connect to the imager. The latter approach was called a software RIP.

Configurable PostScript Interpreter (CPSI)

CPSI (Configurable PostScript Interpreter) from Adobe is the basis for many RIPs from many vendors. It is guaranteed to be fully PostScript Level 2-compatible since it comes from Adobe. Developers can set it up to generate output for specific output devices, such as imagesetters, color proofers, laser printers, high-speed printers, large-format imagesetters, plotters, and computer-to-plate devices. CPSI can be modified to drive a complete range of PostScript devices. CPSI uses the host work-station's operating system and can be used in RIPs for Macintosh, Power Macintosh, SPARCstations and Windows NT as well as others. Although the core of the RIP is CPSI, each RIP vendor has its own user interface and device drivers. The user interface lets you tell the RIP how you want jobs output: you want to use 2,400 dpi, produce a negative image, have pages automatically color-separated, and have the imagesetter punch each page (if it can). The user interface provides you with status information: Job 1 took 4 minutes 10 seconds to RIP and contained no PostScript errors, as an example.

In 1991, Adobe introduced PixelBurst, a NuBus-based card coprocessor with an application-specific integrated circuit (ASIC) that speeds PostScript processing by freeing up the main CPU more quickly, accelerating halftone screening and genera-tion of text and line art—particularly at high resolutions or when outputting large images.

Since its introduction in 1985 when Adobe PostScript software helped spawn the desktop publishing revolution, Adobe has continued to drive the industry forward with powerful printing solutions. The current version of the PostScript page description language developed by Adobe is publicly available to software and RIP developers. This has led to its adoption and recognition as a virtual industry standard. Although Adobe created the original specification for PostScript and then Level 2, other RIP vendors were the first to ship PostScript Level 2 language com-patible RIPs capable of both high and low resolutions running on all major platforms and operating systems. Some non-Adobe RIPs already have features which have not been announced as part of PostScript Level 3, such as support for symmetrical multiprocessing (SMP), TIFF/IT-P1 input format processing, integrated color management, and PostScript display list access and editing.

PostScript Level 3

In September 1996, Adobe Systems Incorporated announced its newest printing systems solution, which includes the next generation of Adobe PostScript called Level 3. Adobe's integrated printing system solution focuses on changing the printing experience by allowing OEM customers to build best-in-class printing solutions and providing users the ability to print complex graphics and Web content, when and where they need it. Adobe has gone beyond offering a page description language to providing a total systems solution for delivering and printing digital documents.

Adobe has developed an advanced level of functionality in Adobe PostScript Level 3 to accommodate the new digital document creation process which includes varying sources, complex composition and virtually unlimited destinations. Users are now accessing content for use in digital documents from varying sources including electronic mail, Web pages, Intranets, on-line services, content providers and digital cameras. Document composition now includes not only text, but also complex graphics, clip art, corporate logos, Internet content, multiple fonts, scanned images and color. Finally, the digital document's destination can be to printing systems anywhere in the world, such as personal printers, network printers, service bureaus, pay for print providers, or data warehouses for electronic archival.

Enhanced Image Technology insures that documents print faster, easier, and with optimal quality. A key benefit to the user is that Enhanced Image Technology recognizes image objects and automatically optimizes processing to deliver the highest possible quality, and at the same time speed return to application. Adobe PostScript Level 3 will include new imaging features that support the increasingly complex documents available via

The genesis of Adobe PostScript Level 3 has been a result of three market trends:
- *the pervasiveness of the Internet*
- *the increasing use of color*
- *a shifting workflow model from print and distribute to distribute and print-on-demand.*

the Internet, support for three-dimensional images, photo quality grayscaling, smooth gradients in graphic objects, image compositing and full-color spectrums.

Adobe PostScript Level 3 with *Advanced Page Processing* increases the performance of an imaging system. As components in a document become more complex, the printing system will process each component as a separate object in order to optimize imaging throughput. PostScript Level 3 will support direct processing of Web content, including HTML and PDF. Advanced Page Processing will also extend the resident font set to provide compatibility with the resident fonts of all leading operating systems, enhancing performance by reducing font downloading. PostScript Level 3 provides users with a more robust ability to manage individual pages within a document, thereby improving control over the printing process.

Adobe's *NetWorks System* improves ease of use, ease of connection and ease of printer management all in one environment through Adobe PostScript Level 3. A printer with NetWorks functionality will include a printer-based Web page, Web-based printer management, printing directly from the printer's Web page, support for all industry standard remote management technologies, and a single step CD-ROM installer for all drivers, fonts and value-added software. Adobe's NetWorks System ultimately allows users to leverage the power and benefits of the Internet.

Adobe PostScript Level 3 also offers Planet Ready Printing to allow local language needs of users anywhere in the world. Users will easily display and print any language with any PostScript Level 3 printer. OEMs will develop complete imaging systems that are savvy to localized demands of language and usage. Specific features include robust drivers that are tightly integrated into the operating system, be it Microsoft Windows 3.1, Microsoft Windows 95, Microsoft Windows NT or Apple Macintosh, and full support of international font requirements.

Adobe has completed Adobe PostScript Level 3 language feature development and will now begin its system integration process. The product schedule includes two internal quality assurance cycles before system delivery to OEM printing system manufacturers and third party development partners in December 1996. In the second half of 1997 when OEMs begin to deliver Adobe PostScript Level 3-based products, Adobe will disclose the Adobe PostScript Level 3 operators and language specific features.

Supra and the Future of RIPs

The high-speed data requirements of digital presses, large-format film imposetters and computer-to-plate systems demand radical changes in RIP and workflow architectures. Developers are also trying to eliminate PostScript processing bottlenecks and accelerate deadline production times. RIP suppliers have been converting PostScript into contone (CT) and linework (LW) files via proprietary methods or converting PostScript into some editable internal format in an attempt to make the RIPing process more efficient.

There are lots of alternatives out there. Covalent Systems' Job Monitor Protocol is a standard framework for collecting data from jobs as they pass through a series of steps and for transferring the data to business systems. Prepress production environments could collect critical information, such as how much time was spent on image editing at one workstation and color correction at another, and to transfer it to a business system for analysis and billing. All of this is available now if you stick with the selection of proprietary systems and custom interfaces between them. Another proposed standard, CIP3, covers the interaction among processes at the front-end prepress operation, the press and the back-end finishing operation. CIP3 is being promoted by Heidelberg, with the support of other press and finishing-equipment suppliers, in addition to front-end system vendors such as Agfa.

Adobe's contribution to the ideal digital workflow is a printing architecture known as Supra which will use PDF as its backbone. Demands for last-minute changes in pages fosters a concept known as "late binding." RIP developers are working toward a format that allows data to be changed after it has been interpreted by the RIP. These changes take account of different printing or proofing requirements, or nonprint delivery.

Adobe's Supra RIP architecture is a major step in RIP evolution. It is built around a new version of Adobe's Portable Document Format. PostScript is an interpretive programming language, PDF is a compact, noninterpretive format designed for fast imaging to a screen. PDF has lacked the ability to handle high-resolution images easily and to handle screening for print—both of these are included within Supra. Supra also connects Web and print publishing, as both will use the new version of PDF as the plug-in to Netscape's Navigator.

The PostScript of the Red Book is fading away. Supra ensures that PostScript document files can be processed as separate but complete pages. Multi-page jobs can be processed by several RIPs simultaneously. Supra is aimed primarily at high volume applications. So far, 26 firms have said they will support Supra.

Agfa, Autologic and Monotype have already delivered the capability for allocating whole jobs among multiple RIPs and ripped work among multiple imagesetters. The industry is getting excited because of Supra's front-end processing.

Working with PostScript
Not all PostScript is equal; code generated by Photoshop conforms to Document Structuring Conventions (DSC), some from QuarkXPress does not. Page structure can't be easily determined. Supra converts such files automatically into PDF format, allowing separate processing. Supra incorporates both Adobe PostScript language and Adobe Portable Document Format (PDF) for production printers, and Adobe PrintMill, an Intranet-based printing and printer management solution.

When you create a page in QuarkXPress or Pagemaker you are interfacing with the program as displayed on the screen. The GUI describes the page on screen for the user. However, when you click Print, it is PostScript code which defines that page as it is sent to the printer or imagesetter. You can even save the PostScript file to disk and read it (if you can decipher it). But a page described in PostScript is nearly uneditable without an understanding of the programming language itself.

PostScript is a voluminous file format. Placing a single "a" on a QuarkXPress page and "printing" the page to an ASCII file produces at least 16 pages of 10/10 type. Not very editable or digestible for humans, unless you speak geek.

Outputting PostScript

There are three choices for outputting a file from an application:

1. Click Print and send the file to a printer on your in-house network. This is a great option if you're publishing a single copy for yourself. Or even a couple of dozen copies for the staff. What if you want to publish your message to hundreds or thousands via a mass printing process?

2. Send the QuarkXPress file to an outside service, but make sure you send the image files and all of the screen and printer fonts. This file can be changed by the service bureau making its integrity questionable.

This second approach not only opens the door for further unpredictability, but it also raises some tricky legal issues. Due to font licensing, the service bureau must install the fonts you use and/or supply, print your job and immediately remove those fonts from their system. This must be done for each job and each time the file is printed.

What if the service bureau has purchased a license to the same font? For instance, you supply a document which uses Garamond. Whose version of Garamond is it—Adobe's, ITC's, Monotype's or some overnight type house's? If you don't specify and/or the service bureau doesn't have the correct version of your typeface, a font substitution will occur. Possible repercussions of an improper font substitution could be the reflowing of text, sometimes destroying the original design. Or maybe you like Courier, the ultimate font substitution.

3. Save the file to disk as PostScript code, which incorporates the images and fonts, and send it to an output service. This is a viable option if you have a very large external storage device to save all of that PostScript information. (Remember, a single "a" generates 16 pages of PostScript text. Well, that's not really fair, because the 16

pages of code could support many text pages. But, PostScript code is voluminous, never the less.)

A drawback to this method is the lack of "correctability." If the correct page setup options were not chosen at the time of PostScript generation, the page may not reproduce as desired. Often, designers don't know the specifications of the imagesetter or output device of the service bureau. Without this information, specifications regarding page size, crop marks, line screen ruling, and many other variables can't be set. And once the PostScript file for that document is generated, it's too late.

What if only a part of a page or a graphic created in a drawing program needs to be placed into a page layout application like QuarkXPress or Pagemaker? Thus was born the Encapsulated PostScript file—a file representing one page with, or in the early days without, a preview image. This allows you to save a graphic in a standardized form and place it into a composite document where it can be scaled and manipulated to fit. However, the EPS file does not save font data and many artists have seen their beautiful graphics output with Courier because the original font was not available at the RIP. So, the EPS was portable only to a point.

PostScript Conclusions
As a platform independent page description language, PostScript has emerged as a de facto standard. Today, PostScript accounts for 95% of the final output of all commercial publications. On the downside, PostScript is extremely variable and page-dependent.

There's no doubt that PostScript has brought on revolutionary advances. But with every revolution comes the need for further refinement. Even Adobe admits that PostScript has many deficiencies for the role it is currently playing. The use of PostScript has far surpassed Adobe's original intention, and thus, they are in the midst of solving problems and advancing their core technology in order to fulfill the expectations of today's digital workflow demands. The wide variety of applications, platforms and typefaces has caused many headaches for the publishing industry. There are just too many places for things to go wrong.

While you can easily move documents around by E-mail, network, or disk, you can't assume that everybody has the right fonts on their system, or that they have the right program to open your document, or even (in a cross-platform environment) the right setup to receive the document. You could spend a lot of time and money installing the same software and fonts, plus the requisite extra hard-disk space and RAM, on every system to allow document portability—and then train people on each program used to create the documents in the first place. But of course, this setup is inefficient and you don't have the capital to implement it, and neither does anyone else.

Actually most of us don't need the job "yesterday." We need it "two weeks ago."

PostScript serves its purpose as a way to describe document pages in a design-rich fashion. But in today's world of ever increasing efficiency, the need for speed, and the customer's insistence on jobs being printed "yesterday," research and development into document handling is a neverending process. Files need to be transferred from place to place quickly, predictably, and efficiently. With the increasing use of digital presses, CTP technology, and completely digital workflows, the need for a platform-independent digital file transfer standards is becoming more and more necessary.

That brings us to the fourth alternative for communicating with graphic service providers amd the outside world, the Portable Document Format. To understand its application value, we move to the next chapter.

CHAPTER

AN INTRODUCTION TO PDF

The Evolution

Simultaneous to the printing and publishing industry's search for an ideal digital document, several software companies claimed they had the answer to paper documents needlessly killing trees, piling up unused in warehouses or filing cabinets, and causing frustration among business people lost in the sea of paper. With the increasing attention being given to the Internet, the idea of a paperless world seemed tangible.

What is a Portable Document?

The underlying concept of document portability is that of printing to a file. As an analogy, take a sheet of paper with text and graphics on it and fax it. The sending fax converts the page images to dots and the receiving fax prints them out. If you have fax capability from your computer, a program takes the page image, converts it to dots and sends it to the printer. Now, save the last file we created—a representation of the page as dots—and instead of printing it to paper, put it on the screen. This document can be sent, viewed, and digested on screen by a large audience without any hint or mention of paper.

But there is something missing. Like any fax image, there is no underlying *intelligence* for the text. You could not search through

Portable documents are self-reliant files that remain intact regardless of the platform they were created on. In other words they can be moved electronically from computer to computer, for viewing or printing, and retain their content and format integrity.

it because it does not know an *'a'* from a hole in the paper. Searchability is something you want.

Some portable documents save a bitmap of the page as it appears on the screen, the underlying ASCII text, and the font data. By having the text in ASCII format you can search for words and phrases. This is a major advantage over print. After all, the material in a book or catalog is not really information until you find what you want.

A drawback to portable documents is analogous to some of the portable TVs of the 1950s when you had a unit that weighed hundreds of pounds with a handle on the top. Even with compression, some portable documents are six to ten times bigger than the original application file. True, the final file size is larger than the original application file counterpart, but the advantage is quite significant.

By creating an electronic document that carries all the needed components—fonts, graphics, and even a program to view and print the document—portable document software could eliminate the cost and time of printing, distributing, and storing paper copies, while adding the ability to find text and link multiple documents so information would be more accessible and more dynamic.

Whether for use within a company for document exchange and distribution, or for use on bulletin-board systems, CD-ROMs, or fax-back services for user-requested documents, the possibilities for portable-document software were beguiling.

The Portable Document Enters the Market
In 1990, developers introduced portable document software. First came No Hands Software's Common Ground. Adobe later shipped Acrobat and Farallon Computing followed with Replica. Other companies also had their version of portable document formats.

Adobe's Portable Document
Adobe Systems dove into the competition in 1993 defining their Portable Document Format as a file format used to represent a

---

Acrobat Distiller
Acrobat Distiller is used to convert any PostScript file into the Portable Document Format (PDF). Distilling a file is the best option when dealing with complex information such as high-resolution images, gradients, and other artwork. The result is a page-independent, highly-structured, small file size format ready for delivery. Acrobat Reader allows for viewing, navigating, and printing a distilled document.

Acrobat Reader
Reader's role is primarily for viewing as well as third party proofing and approving. The client can retrieve a PDF via the Internet, view it and approve it without having the original application program. Adobe has made the Reader free and downloadable at www.adobe.com

Acrobat Exchange
Acrobat Exchange is also for viewing; however, editing features are included. Hyperlinking, bookmarking, deletion and insertion of pages, and password protection are all possible. Version 3.0 has also added word editing.

document independent of the application software, hardware, and operating system used to create it. The software used to create this PDF was called Acrobat (actually, its original name was "Carousel").

Adobe's PDF was a third version of a PostScript file format. It took the PostScript file of the document and ripped it (called distilling) to a new format that saved every page as an individual item, compressed the type and images and cut out almost all the variability of the programming language. What remained was a portable document file that could be viewed on almost any platform, Mac or PC, running DOS, Windows, MacOS or UNIX. But the first version of Adobe Acrobat did not fully support high-end printing for color separations.

The PostScript code needed for production printing was not included. This did not hinder the use of PDFs to view on monitors or to print to monochrome and color printers, but it was not able to output, for example, a composite CMYK file as four monochrome PostScript streams to be sent to an imagesetter.

The Ultimate Portability

The printing and publishing industry saw more potential in the PDF than just looking at pages on a screen. Like the success of PostScript itself, the success of the PDF was based on capturing the high end of the printing world. Competitors to Acrobat only saw viewing as the problem to be solved. They forgot that paper was and always will be the only form of communicating to everyone in the world regardless of their lifestyle or location. Paper is the only democratic form of communication, since it does not restrict access because of technology.

Towards the Ideal Digital Document

Adobe acknowledged the need to meet the demands of the high-end printing market. As a result of their working relationships with organizations such as the PDF Group and DDAP, Acrobat is emerging as the software capable of creating the near ideal digital document.

The printing and publishing market expressed their needs, and Adobe listened. Acrobat 3.0 was released in November 1996

PDF Components
PDF files contain: a view file that displays the page as you created it, embedded type (Type 1 and TrueType), graphic objects (bitmaps and vector images), links for variable forms data and links to sound and QuickTime or AVI movies.

PDF Group
A professional group of representatives from leading production and printing companies who have joined in support of the PDF in the areas of electronic delivery and pre-press workflow. The group members are working directly with Adobe to solve problems as well as provide input for necessary additions.

DDAP
Stands for The Digital Distribution of Advertising for Publications. Started in 1991 as an ad-hoc industry committee to implement various industry standards. Today DDAP is active in the role of including PDF as an industry standard.

with added functions necessary for the high-end market. Acrobat 3.0 incorporates extended graphics state functions so that color separation can occur more effectively and OPI image comments can now be preserved. The PDF pages can be exported as an EPS for insertion in a page makeup program, like QuarkXPress or PageMaker—only this time the font data is saved.

The Ideal Digital Document

As presented in the previous chapter, the choices for moving documents from place to place are few and not very attractive. Thanks to Acrobat, we have an alternative to sharing large, bulky, and arbitrary information containers.

Imagine an ideal digital document. How many headaches would be avoided if there was a portable, page-independent, platform independent file format which could not only preserve design richness, but also allow for repurposability, searchability, predictability, and even some editability? This ideal digital document describes the Portable Document Format. PDF may not only be the aspirin for your headaches, but may also very well be the refinement of the PostScript revolution. PDF documents:

- Preserve design richness
- Create predictability
- Maintain some editability
- Create searchability
- Allow repurposability

Design Richness

Preserving design richness entails maintaining the look and feel from creation to final output by properly reproducing all content information within the document such as bitmap, vectored line art, and text. In order to understand the complexity of preserving design richness, a few definitions are needed:

Bitmap or raster images

A bitmap image is an image which is defined digitally by a number of pixels in a rectangular array. Because computers are binary entities they must break up images into a map of small pieces, called picture elements, or pixels. All images that are

Bitmap (Scanned) Line Art

scanned into a computer are bitmap images whether black and white line drawings, or black and white or color photos.

Monochrome bitmap images are the simplest and the smallest in file size. Scanned black and white line drawings are monochrome bitmaps. Each pixel of the bitmap can either be black or white (on or off), so only two bits of computer information are required to define these bitmaps. For this reason, they are also called bilevel bitmaps.

Grayscale bitmaps are a step above monochrome bitmaps because instead of 1 bit per pixel, they contain 8 bits per pixel. Eight-bit images can then yield 256 levels of gray. Because more bits are used for each pixel, grayscale images are larger in file size than monochrome images.

Grayscale Contone

Color bitmap images can be either 24-bit (RGB) or 32-bit (CMYK) yielding millions of possible color combinations for each pixel. Thus, color bitmap file sizes tend to be very large, humongous even.

Because the human eye cannot discern the individual pixels, we perceive the images to be smooth lines (monochrome bitmaps) or continuous tone (grayscale and color bitmaps). These digital images can accurately describe an original image, but tend to be very large in file size.

Line art

Line art is described as a combination of lines, curves, tints and fills in vector form to allow it to be scaled, rotated, etc. and converted to a very compact version of the data that is independent of the final size of the image.

Vector-based line art

Unlike bitmap images which are defined in terms of pixels, vector images are defined by the curves used to create the shape. (Remember all that ugly geometry: $y = x^2 + 2$)? Think of it as lots of little electronic rubber bands which are anchored at some points and pulled apart at others.

Text

Text is carried as character symbols with placement information, which can be converted to the final image through use of font drawing information. This allows the size of the text, and the font used to be varied during the creative process.

PostScript allows users to design and create pages containing bitmaps, line art, and text without concern for a particular platform or output device. Acrobat Distiller transforms PostScript files from PC, Macintosh, and UNIX systems into all-inclusive bundles retaining all formatting, graphics and photographic images that the original documents contain.

Portability

Document portability is our concern. Computer users have suffered from a lack of formatted text, loss of graphics and lack of proper fonts installed on particular computers that are used to view and print documents. Documents have been somewhat portable through the use of ASCII and Rich Text Format (RTF) files, but content alone does not always convey the true message without formatting.

PDF*ing* a file makes it "portable" across computer platforms. A PDF file is a 7-bit ASCII file, and uses only the printable subset of the ASCII character set to describe documents—even those with images and special characters. As a result, PDF files are extremely portable even across diverse hardware and operating system environments.

Furthermore, PDF provides a new solution that makes a document independent of the fonts used to create it. Fonts can either be embedded or descriptors can be used. Embedding the fonts in the PostScript stage includes the actual font outlines in the file. Distilling this file will ensure that pages are displayed with type characters in exact position. The font descriptor includes the font name, character metrics, and style information. This is the information needed to simulate missing fonts and is typically only 1–2K per font. If a font used in a document is available on the computer where the document is viewed, it is used. If it is not available, two Adobe Multiple Master fonts are used to simulate on a character-by-character basis the weight and width of the original font, to maintain the overall color and formatting of the original document.

ASCII

The American Standard Code for Information Interchange is the most basic coding system for text and serves as the foundation for virtually every system that encodes information. Almost every document can be saved as ASCII which can then be imported to any other document.

Rich Text Format (RTF)

Microsoft format used to go across platform with fonts, style sheets and graphics to some extent. Once thought to be a portable document format but it was not robust (rich?) enough.

Font embedding does add some size to the document; however, it provides an important aspect of document portability—cross-platform font fidelity and the ability to printout at any resolution. This means that the receiver of the digital page could have a high resolution color printer and print out pages as needed at a remote location. Pages could be created in one part of the world and then sent to a printer in the opposite hemisphere who uses the data to make high resolution films for printing.

The PDF provides a solution to three information needs:
- *The need for an interchange format for viewing richly formatted documents.*
- *The need for a data format for archiving documents.*
- *A format for transmitting documents for remote printing.*

Editability
Last-minute changes to a PDF can be made via a new plug-in for Acrobat Exchange. Since the PDF is vector-based and includes the font name, character metrics, and style information, small type changes are possible. Full paragraphs cannot be edited due to the lack of reflow capabilities, but those small yet sometimes crucial changes such as misspelled words or incorrect phone numbers or prices can be made on a last-minute basis within Acrobat Exchange.

Predictability
Acrobat PDF eliminates the variability of PostScript and provides a foundation for effective digital print production workflow. A RIP interprets PostScript, converts it into a display list of page objects and then rasterizes the page into a map of on/off dots that drive the marking engine. When you distill a document into a PDF you are essentially doing the interpretation and display list functions as in the RIP process.

The resulting PDF is a database of objects that appear on a page and how they relate to each other—a print-specific file with extensions for OPI, image screening information and more. The variability of PostScript is squeezed out and only the essence remains—which can be output back into the PostScript stream again for printout. If your document can be distilled to a PDF, the odds are that it will output reliably on any PostScript RIP.

Searchability
With the Acrobat software, it is possible to find information instantly. There is a full-text search tool which allows the user to retrieve exactly what they need. Hypertext links can be used to simplify browsing and navigation features such as bookmarks

*PDF is not your father's
PostScript.*
*PDF defines basic types of objects,
such as numbers, names, arrays,
dictionaries and streams. Page descriptions, outlines, annotations and
thumbnails are built from these objects, as in PostScript. Objects have
an object number and a generation
number, allowing multiple versions
of an object to exist within a document. The object can be referenced
indirectly by its object number.*

*PDF operators are mostly one letter,
unlike the verbose PostScript operators. Several operators combine
more than one PostScript operation.
The 'b' operator in PDF does the
work of PostScript's closepath, fill
and stroke verbs, as an example.*

*PDF does not have programming
constructions for branching (if . . .
else) or looping. The PDF interpreter runs straight through the
code when it displays or prints.*

*The pages of a file may not follow
each other in sequence and are
accessed through a catalog/balanced-
tree data structure, analogous to a
disk directory system.*

*When versions of a file are saved, a
new table is appended to the end of
the file and contains a pointer to the
previous cross-reference table to
trace back through earlier versions.*

*A PDF file contains a cross-refer-
ence table of objects which can be
used to quickly find the data needed
to display a page. The table allows
different pages to share data. As
annotations are created and erased,
the table is updated.*

and cross-documentation links are also included to help the
user move through numerous documents faster.

Repurposability

Adobe's PDF for some time has been marketed as a Web tool
offering greater design richness over the HTML language constraints. PDFs can be downloaded to the World Wide Web and
accessed through the free Acrobat Reader plug-in. A document
created for print output and distilled into a PDF can now, with
virtually no changes, be used on a website. This means that sites
can now be created with all design richness available in PLAs
such as QuarkXPress and Pagemaker.

PDF and PostScript

Although PDF files require PostScript information to be created,
the resulting PDF files are different from their PostScript counterpart. A PDF file is not a PostScript language program and
cannot be directly interpreted by a PostScript interpreter.
However, the page descriptions in a PDF file can be converted
into a PostScript file.

How PDF Files Work

The PDF file format is not a programming language like
PostScript. You cannot send a PDF file to a laser printer directly
because the file format contains information that a PostScript
RIP would not understand. The PDF does contain PostScript
code, but the extra PDF data would inhibit the RIP from processing the document. A PDF file must be sent to a RIP through
the Acrobat Reader or Exchange application. When read by
Reader, the PDF is converted into a PostScript file and sent to
the RIP just like any other PostScript file.

Creating a PDF File

The two methods for creating PDF are:
- PDFWriter
- Acrobat Distiller

The PDFWriter, available on both Apple Macintosh computers
and computers running the Microsoft Windows environment,
acts as a printer driver. The PDFWriter shows up as a printer in
the Macintosh Chooser window. The user needs to choose that

"printer" to create a PDF file. The user then "prints" their file to the PDFWriter and an electronic file is produced. This is similar to "print to disk."

For more complex documents that involve high resolution images and detailed illustrations, the PDF file must be created differently because of limitations of PDFWriter. Acrobat Distiller was developed for this situation. Distiller produces PDF files from PostScript files that have been "printed to disk." The Distiller application accepts any PostScript file, whether created by a program or hand-coded. Distiller produces more efficient PDF files than PDFWriter for various reasons.

Viewing and Editing PDF Files

You can view a PDF file with Acrobat Exchange and Acrobat Reader. Acrobat Reader is a free downloadable file available from Adobe at [www.adobe.com]. Copies of the reader can be shared with others. These two applications contain the interface that allows users to easily navigate through a PDF document, even those that contain thousands of pages.

To improve performance for interactive viewing, a PDF defines a more structured format than that used by most PostScript language programs. PDF also includes objects, such as annotations and hypertext links, that are not part of the page itself but are useful for interactive viewing.

In the Workplace

The PDF workflow has already been embraced by the printing and publishing industry with some very successful results. The Associated Press has developed something called AP Adsend. You create a newspaper ad on a Macintosh or PC and save it as a PostScript file, distill it into a PDF file, fill out an on-screen delivery ticket specifying which newspapers are to run it and when, then transmit it in compressed form to the AP.

They then distribute it directly to the designated newspaper or newspapers. The ad is received by the newspaper's computer looking just the way you created it. They position it into their desktop layout file for the issue. There is no ad film and no overnight delivery.

Differences between PostScript and PDF

- *A PDF file may contain objects such as hypertext links that are useful only for interactive viewing.*

- *To simplify the processing of page descriptions, PDF provides no programming language constructs.*

- *PDF enforces a strictly defined file structure that allows an application to access parts of a document randomly.*

- *PDF files contain information such as font metrics, to ensure viewing fidelity.*

- *PDF requires files to be represented in ASCII, to enhance document portability.*

About Adobe Acrobat

- *View documents with guaranteed page fidelity. It is not necessary for the user to buy the application. The Reader is free.*

- *Time is saved by sending information and files over E-mail.*

- *Collateral and technical documentation can be stored electronically and accessed instantly. This is helpful with sales and customer service groups.*

Creating, Using & Distributing PDF

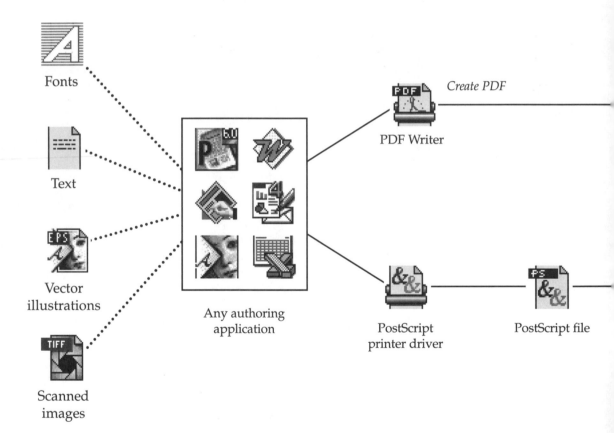

Fonts

Text

Vector
illustrations

Scanned
images

Any authoring
application

Create PDF

PDF Writer

PostScript
printer driver

PostScript file

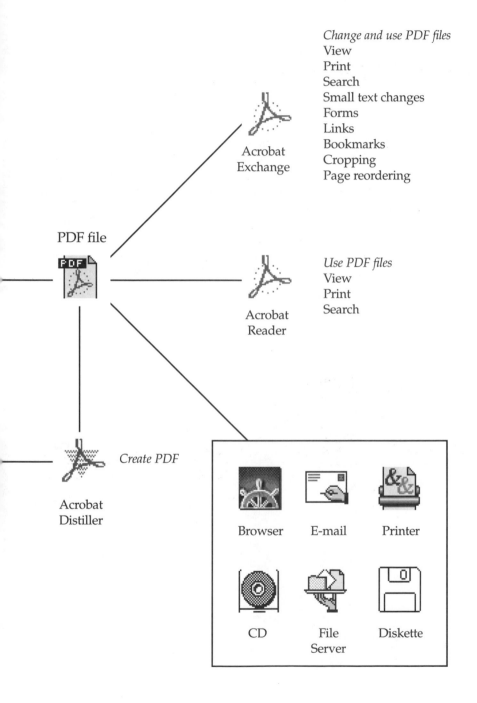

Change and use PDF files
View
Print
Search
Small text changes
Forms
Links
Bookmarks
Cropping
Page reordering

Acrobat
Exchange

PDF file

Use PDF files
View
Print
Search

Acrobat
Reader

Create PDF

Acrobat
Distiller

Browser   E-mail   Printer

CD   File   Diskette
            Server

This technology goes beyond the transmission of newspaper ads. It allows access to entire electronic archives of information. The browsing, searching and reading possibilities are extensive. It is a giant step for document independence, where software creates a giant electronic "manila envelope" filled with just about anything from pages to sound to video. With cross-platform interoperability and sufficient bandwidth for video/audio transmission, an advertiser will be able to send ads and or commercials directly to publications, broadcast media, or even directly to online service subscribers.

For newspaper and magazine publishers the digital distribution of advertising is a critical issue. They must have every part of the publication in digital form to take advantage of direct-to imposed film or plate.

CHAPTER

PRINT-RELATED PROCESSES & ISSUES

Now that we have reviewed how the Portable Document Format becomes a predictable, platform-independent, page-independent entity which solves many of the limitations of PostScript, we must tackle other print-related workflow issues. Issues such as trapping, imposition and OPI play an important role in the success of PDF as a link to the completely digital workflow for the high-end printing and publishing world.

The very essence of digital workflow for printing and publishing involves the integration of many process steps. The most common processes include:
- Preflighting
- Trapping
- OPI serving
- Imposition

Each of these steps has evolved from manual techniques to computer operation with manual intervention and now totally automated approaches. For a long time each step often required a different server to perform a function or functions. The trend today is toward more comprehensive and cohesive systems that are transparent to the user.

Trapping

Trapping can take place at the application program level, at a separate computer with dedicated trapping software, or at the RIP equipped with trapping functionality.

Trapping Approaches

Automating the analysis process for a PostScript file has two approaches.

- The first approach parses the PostScript code to identify the logical objects on the page (text strings, tint blocks, contone images, line drawings, and other objects) and their relationships to each other. It works with geometric properties, and is called the vector method.
- The second approach rasterizes the file and then analyzes at the resulting raster image to determine where colors are adjacent—called the raster method.
- Hybrid systems use a combination of vector and raster technologies.

Each approach works. Vector-based trapping is a mathematical masterpiece and works well with PostScript which is a geometric, vector-oriented method of describing a page. Analyzing the objects to be trapped should be simpler from a vector viewpoint. The output of a standalone trapping product (if it is also PostScript code) for most pages will be more compact if it is derived from an object description rather than a rasterized bitmap. That, in turn, reduces the transmission and processing time for the RIP that will receive the code.

Once the objects have been identified within the trapping program, sometimes relatively little mathematical manipulation is required to generate the chokes or spreads needed, and it's just a matter of changing the width and depth of an object according to a set of formulas. (When objects cross over multiple colors, then a new PostScript trap object is generated with its own width and depth. Here, more arithmetic is required.) With complex object outlines, such as serif type, vector trapping is more effective in generating the smaller trap outlines for type without losing its defining shape. Part of this is because sharp corners can be regenerated mathematically with precision, better than a raster approach that might round off corners.

One type of PostScript data that resists vector analysis is scanned images. These are truly raster data, so vector-oriented trapping programs must look at the pixel values to determine the color value of the trap. To trap to a vignette or a photographic image, there are two approaches:
- determine an average value for the entire image,
- figure the traps on a pixel-by-pixel basis (often known as sliding traps).

Using either approach requires some level of analysis of the raster data. Vector approaches can bog down when there are lots of tiny objects on the page because of the need to generate and process the many tiny objects needed to create the trap areas.

Raster-based trapping algorithms have been refined to the point that they can be executed very quickly. A raster file is the least common denominator for any page once separated into plates, it is very easily converted into screened bitmaps, the ultimate form for any page when it goes to a raster output device. Raster-based algorithms should not have to redo the rasterization process and should find it equally easy to work with any number or combination of objects on the page. Raster approaches generate gobs of binary data. The interim data structures tend to need lots of RAM and disk space, and the results can take a long time to output. This is not quite the problem it used to be, as disks and chips get cheaper by the hour, and data compression techniques improve. High-end prepress systems have always done trapping by analyzing raster data.

Hybrid trapping uses combinations of vector and raster analysis. Some approaches rasterize the file at relatively low resolution to locate object boundaries and color combinations. They use this knowledge to create new objects containing the trap colors, which are then output as a series of PostScript objects These objects are then merged with the original EPS file and sent to be ripped. Hybrid approaches sometimes end up rasterizing the file at two different resolutions in two different machines which could lead to noticeable trapping problems.

No mathematical program can anticipate all design situations and corrections, and some of these situations must be made at the source application, while others can be done in the trapping program. The more changes that can be made in an automatic trapping program, the more efficient the resulting workflow will be.

Some Trapping Functions:
- Trap color and placement based on components of adjacent colors.
- Trapping of blends with sliding traps for smooth transitions.
- On-screen preview of all trap locations and colors.
- Unlimited trap zones to confine a trap area or apply different parameters.
- Integrated batch-processing capability.
- Trap-conforming EPS files or multipage PostScript files, from anywhere, to anywhere.
- Correctly spread light into dark colors, and achieve optimal colors and placement.
- Increase productivity by outputting files immediately after trapping is complete.
- Maximum control trapping bitmap and continuous tone images against other objects.
- Evaluate and adjust the traps you want before you commit to page or imposed film.
- Trap only the areas that need it, or alter parameters based on custom requirements.
- Set parameters for each file to be trapped; leave file unattended during processing.

In-RIP Trapping

A while back, Mitch Bogart, the technical genius at Rampage, emphasized that trapping functionality should be moved to the RIP. Some people have argued against such a move, claiming that, if the trapping took place in the RIP, you wouldn't be able to check the trapping before you have printed on the press. As long as a RIP takes input in a standard form (EPS files for example) and output is in standard form, a RIP should be considered open rather than closed and proprietary. Trapping may also be handled faster and better when integrated with the RIP. There are other functions such as screening that are also best left integrated. What about spot color separation, JPEG decompression, and OPI replacement? There is a technical synergy that comes from grouping functions together. It also removes the burden for many of these tasks from the originator.

Regarding proofing, the mistake lies in thinking of a RIP as an invisible black box that comes glued to each output device. Not only is this more expensive, since each output device, proofer and printer must have its own RIP, but, as many have pointed out, the multiplicity of RIPs leads to inevitable visual fidelity problems. Different rippings produce different results. This is especially true when dealing with OPI replacement, fonts, spot colors and other enhancements for high-quality, high-speed production RIPs. Instead one should view the RIP as a sort of central workstation, taking in files and outputting to the screen and multiple peripherals. Before, the RIP was part of a system; now, the RIP is the system. However, Supra and PDF change the concept a tad. Visual fidelity is assured because the PDF captures the page with more data about the page and the same RIP architecture is used.

Adobe has a PostScript interpreter which incorporates built-in trapping of color pages with a patented, state-of-the-art in-RIP trapping technology. Trapping of color pages is the process of micro-adjusting images on multicolor output devices to compensate for physical limitations of printing presses and other reproduction systems. Adobe expects to license to OEM customers the Adobe PostScript interpreter software with built-in trapping capabilities. Two of Adobe's printing system manufacturer customers, Agfa Division of Bayer, Inc., and Crosfield Electronics Ltd., demonstrated in-RIP trapping technology in September 1996.

Imposition
One area in the prepress industry that has developed rapidly in the past couple of years is electronic imposition. Due to the prevalence of large-format imagesetters and platesetters, many users are turning to imposition programs for workflow automation. Some imposition functions:
- Standard and custom imposition layouts for sheet or web printing.
- Form, file, and page-level positioning and rotation, with

verso/recto page controls.
- Enhanced shingling and bottling controls.
- Customizable page, and sheet marks, with the option to use EPS art as a mark.
- On-screen preview of press sheets, with all marks and pages in place and proportion.
- Support for pin-registration systems with full control over form and sheet position.
- Impose PostScript files from any application or platform, output them to any device.
- Accommodate all standard binding methods, as well as irregular layouts.
- Gain maximum control by applying parameters by the job, file, or page.
- Achieve highest degree of accuracy when compensating for folding discrepancies.
- Modify any printer's mark to meet particular production requirements.
- Check the accuracy and placement of all parts of a form before output.
- Accurate placement of imposition forms for plate-ready film or press-ready plates.
- Send, impose, and return pre-trapped files for separation without intervention.

OPI

Aldus' Open Prepress Interface (now under Adobe) has become a generic term meaning low-resolution picture replacement. PageMaker users wanted a simple way to use high-res color photos that had been scanned on high-end scanners, without having the data burden that accompanies those images. Aldus decided it made more sense to use PageMaker to design the layout and compose the text, then add a few commands to tell the output system how to position the color files. They were right.

OPI is an extension of the PostScript language and was developed by Aldus Corporation. OPI workflows can improve prepress system performance by reducing the amount of data that workstations and networks must carry and process. An OPI Server keeps high resolution graphics stored until imagesetter or printer or platemaker output time, and creates a low resolution "view file" for applications to work with. The preview is sometimes called:

- a proxy image
- an FPO (For Position Only)
- a view file
- a screen view file
- a placement file.

An OPI Server adds the ability to "OPI-Publish" TIFF images from the Server database. For each high-resolution TIFF image which is "OPI- Published," a view file (a low-resolution version of the same image) is made available. When users of OPI-compatible applications need TIFF graphics, they can use these view files instead of the actual high-resolution graphics. Since the view files may contain fewer than 75 pixels per inch (compared with high-resolution TIFF contones with up to 300 samples per inch or line art with up to 1,000 samples per inch), much less data is transmitted and processed in the workstation.

The computer operates faster, since these view files contain much less graphic data, but users can still see each graphic on the screen and can scale, crop, rotate, etc., as if it were an actual high resolution graphic. These low-res "placement only" files contain information about where the high-resolution file is located, how the image has been scaled, cropped and rotated. This information is in the form of OPI comments within the low-resolution file. At output time, the application creates a PostScript file with image processing instructions (OPI Comments) substituted for each OPI view file. The OPI Server scales, crops, rotates, and merges the high-resolution images with the PostScript file according to these instructions.

Macintosh users can access OPI features only via OPI-compatible applications such as QuarkXPress or Adobe PageMaker. OPI operation with these applications is identical to standard operation with two exceptions:

- Some functions are faster, due to the smaller quantity of graphic data that is being handled by the computer.
- To output an item containing OPI view files, or to place it in the Server database, a Macintosh user "saves" it as an EPS file in a Server folder, with TIFF images omitted.

Sometimes two Server folders are set up for this purpose—one for direct output and one for storage in the Server database. QuarkXPress also offers an alternate method for OPI output in which the user can "save as EPS" with TIFF omitted.

For direct output, the OPI merging function (part of the OPI Server) receives the PostScript file, integrates the high-resolution image from the database, and performs scaling, cropping, and rotation as directed in the OPI comments before automatically outputting the entire job to the PostScript device. OPI resolves the problem of large image files and deals with the data burden that impedes productivity.

The OPI industry-standard convention defines how to embed instructions in a PostScript output file to tell the output device where and how to merge the various text and graphics components of a page. OPI enables users to work with low-res preview

Image workflow with OPI

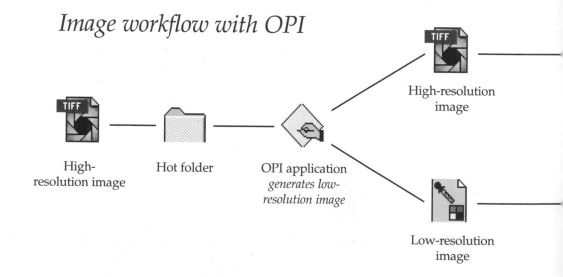

High-resolution image

High-resolution image

Hot folder

OPI application
generates low-resolution image

Low-resolution image

images in their page-makeup programs, and keep the high-res graphic images close to the imagesetter. This maximizes workstation productivity and minimizes network traffic.

Working with OPI

Pre-1: Send your images to a service bureau or printer and have them scan them and provide you with the low-res screen images while they maintain the high-res print images on their OPI Server.

1. Make up pages using any of a variety of desktop publishing applications. Compose and assemble the editorial content, line art, charts, ads, and other page elements.
2. Place low-res OPI images on the page using a preview image, which is a low-resolution TIFF image.
3. Send the job to the service bureau or printer for output.
4. The OPI server, reads the path name, fetches the high-res image from the Server, and merges the image in position with the text and other elements.

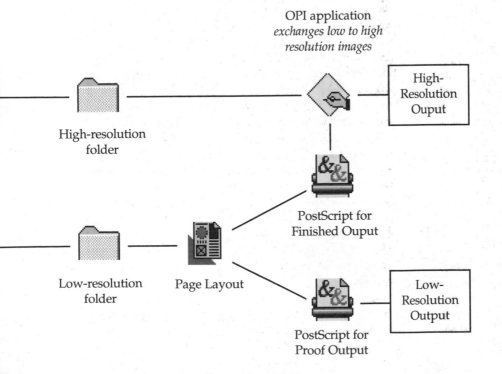

OPI application
*exchanges low to high
resolution images*

High-Resolution Ouput

High-resolution
folder

PostScript for
Finished Ouput

Low-resolution
folder

Page Layout

PostScript for
Proof Output

Low-Resolution Output

The high-res image resides at or near the RIP or RIP Server or the network Server, and its storage path and file name must match the storage path and file name on the Server. Many vendors offer OPI solutions that support TIFF, EPS or DCS files. Most all support all the cropping and sizing commands issued in the page makeup program. When the page makeup program creates a PostScript output file of the job for the printer, it appends these commands, along with the path name and file name, as PostScript comments in the job stream. When the OPI-compliant output device reads these comments, it acts upon them by retrieving and merging the high-res image.

DCS and OPI

Many OPI solutions also support DCS (Desktop Color Separation), another standardized convention for handling color separations created with desktop publishing programs. DCS originated with Quark Inc. as a way to manage color separation files. In general, DCS is a subset of the EPS file format. In producing color separations, DCS-compliant programs such as Photoshop generate a set of five EPSF files. These five files include a main, or "composite" file, as well as a file for each color separation: cyan, magenta, yellow, and black. The composite file contains the names of the cyan, magenta, yellow, and black EPS files and the path name to their storage location, PostScript commands to print a non-separated version of the image, and a 72-dpi PICT version of the image for viewing on the screen. DCS 2.0 offers easier maintenance by offering a single file format which contains all of this information.

In a typical DCS operation, the user places the composite image in the Quark file. When the user prints the job, Quark sends the color separations instead of the composite image. OPI systems that also support DCS enhance this operation by allowing the color separation files to be stored on the Server, so Quark does not have to transmit these large color files at print time. Quark sends only the callouts, containing the path name to the separation files, and the OPI Server fetches those files accordingly.

Encapsulated PostScript

PostScript was originally designed only to send files to a printer. But PostScript's ability to scale and translate (move the ori-

DCS (Desktop Color Separation) was originated by QuarkXPress to offer an alternative to OPI/TIFF. It used the five-file EPS format which made EPS into bitmaps for CMYK with a view file.

It might be said that somewhere in the mists of time it was thought that EPS could do what PDFs do. But EPS did not embed font data (which it now does with PDF).

EPS wanted to be what PDF is: a viewable, editable PostScript file.

gin of) what follows makes it possible to embed pieces of PostScript and place them where you want on the page. These pieces are EPS files. EPS is considered a graphic file format.

The PostScript code in an EPS has to follow certain rules. For instance, it shouldn't erase the page since that would affect the whole page, not just its own part. It is forbidden to select a page size, because this would both change the size of, and erase, the whole page.

An EPS file includes a special header made up of PostScript comments (starting with %) which have no effect on a printer. The most important comment is %%Bounding Box. This gives the location of the EPS picture if it is not scaled or translated. A program uses this information to place the picture accurately within a page. The PostScript part of an EPS file is "stripped in" to the PostScript generated as the document is printed, preceded by PostScript "scale" and "translate" instructions.

If you send an EPS file to the printer it might print a copy of the graphic. Or it might print nothing at all. Or a blank page. EPS files aren't designed for printing, but sometimes you get lucky. At the very least, EPS files always print on a default page size since they mustn't include a page size.

When a desktop publishing program uses an EPS graphic, it isn't smart enough to interpret the PostScript in the EPS to show a picture. So, the EPS file is often accompanied by a preview. This is a low-resolution picture the DTP program does know how to show. There are several forms of preview. An EPS file without a preview is still usable but probably shows on screen as a gray box—people expect more than that!

There are three types of preview:
- Macintosh
- DOS
- System independent.

The Macintosh preview is a PICT graphic in the EPS file's resource fork. This means the EPS file's data fork contains just PostScript. The DOS preview is embedded in the file, and there's a special header. A DOS EPS with preview cannot be printed until the header and preview are removed. In DOS, the preview is embedded as a TIFF or WMF graphic.

An EPS file with system-independent preview is called EPSI. This adds a monochrome bitmap as comments inside the file. It isn't really system-independent since on the Macintosh and in DOS many applications don't support it. They can use the file, but won't show the preview.

Many Macintosh programs will read DOS format EPS files, and handle them OK if they contain a TIFF preview. DOS programs can read Macintosh EPS files but they can never see the preview hidden in the resource fork.

Other variations of EPS which may make a file unusable are binary and Level 2. Binary EPS files work well on a Macintosh, but most PCs can't print them, because any Control+D in the data will reset a typical PC PostScript printer. Most EPS files written on a Macintosh are binary and don't work on most PCs. Level 2 EPS files can only be printed on a Level 2 printer.

This little discussion on EPS and related forms was provided to help you understand that we, as an industry, have been struggling to find a universal, standardized format for moving files and documents around networks. The solution is now the PDF. Once documents have made the transition to electronic form and have made their way through a pre-press or pre-publishing system one of the most important steps—and it occurs at various points—is proofing, or the verification of documents prior to printing.

Proofing

"Edging closer to dotlessness" as Seybold Publications describes it, may be the theme in the color proofing area. The contract proof (the verification proof that the client, service bureau, and printer agree will be the standard for color and quality) issue is moving toward an uneasy acceptance. Most contract proofs have used film-based technology, but with the increasing move to all-digital workflows, and as computer-to-plate systems avoid film entirely, film-based proofing is being replaced by proofs from digital data. A contract proof has tradi-

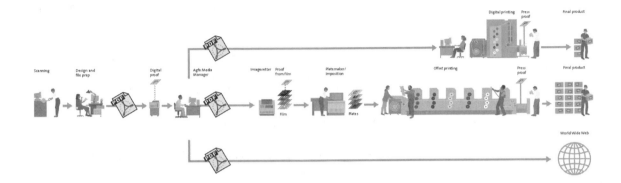

PDF workflow (above) versus parallel workflow (below)

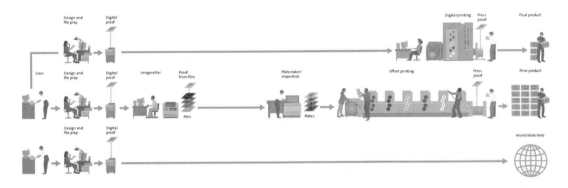

Multiple re-purposing of the same PDF document: Once in Acrobat 3.0 PDF form your document is now free to be anything it needs to be: paper, film, plate, proof, WWW-viewable file, data, document, or image archive, and more. New automated workflow tools will open the PDF, save the pictures in a new form, and redistill the document for another purpose. Or save the pictures into an image database for access by clients as they build documents for different publishing streams. With a totally digital publication you can now go directly to plate or digital press. Drag files over icons representing desired functions and the system does the rest. Files are moved through various operations on their way to uniform and predictable output. PDF workflows are open and non-proprietary. Savings of 50% over conventional digital workflows are predicted.

Conventional workflows force multiple reworking of the same creative elements: Today's digital workflows require many steps and many points of human intervention. To meet the needs of a multitude of clients with different application programs, layout approaches, prepress knowledge, and skill levels, many prepress networks lose the automation that they promised. PDF workflows reduce human interaction. Receiving files from a host of clients applying a host of applications with a host of fonts and a host of EPS or TIFF or CT or other bitmap files, then using the appropriate version of the driver to generate the proper PostScript code to get the printout the client desires has long been a painful, error-prone process. Pre-flighting was born to check the files for missing elements, incorrect settings, and proper procedures.

tionally shown the exact halftone dot structure so that potential printing problems like moiré can be avoided. Some digital proofing systems reproduce halftone dots, and some do not. Print buyers are accepting contract proofs without dots. Screening is now pretty much a non-issue since print buyers seem prepared to accept FM screening and make moiré passé. The contract proof market now appears to be a battle between inkjet and dye sublimation proofers—both without dots.

Most vendors of CTP systems also offer imposition proofers to replicate blueline imposition proofs. These tend to be large-format monochrome plotters, although there are some in color and some that print on both sides of the sheet to show true imposition. Imposition printers, used in conjunction with inkjet, dye sublimation or other proofing engines, are looked at as the future course for digital proofing within new workflows. For people who still want traditional dot proofs (and are willing to pay for them) dot proofers are available. And some users may even keep an imagesetter around to produce film only for proofing purposes in a CTP environment.

Remote Proofing
A major trend is that of remote proofing, where an inkjet or dye sublimation or other color proofer is physically installed in a customer location. PDFs from the customer are sent to the prepress or printing service and processed. The Server system prepares a version of the PDF that calibrates to the eventual reproduction device and the files are returned to the customer for proofing printout. Since the PDF files are compressed, they can be sent via telecommunications lines to and from the customer.

New Servers and RIPs will automatically direct PDFs to queues based on the customer, reproduction device (litho press, flexo press, digital color press, or whatever) and convert or modify files as required for each step in the workflow.

CHAPTER

DIGITAL WORKFLOW ENVIRONMENTS

Discussions of digital workflow always seem to start by showing conventional workflows: scanning, assembly, film output, stripping, contacting exposure, duping, proofing and plate exposure. Since most print-oriented organizations have moved into film imagesettting and imposetting, there are now more users with partial digital workflows than those without them.

Partial digital workflow refers to the fact that most users still have little islands of automation that are not integrated into a comprehensive system. Using network or sneaker-net, they are moving files to specialized servers for specialized operations.

Too often workflows have been constructed around people rather than machines. The trend today—and the PDF is in the forefront of that movement—is to move workflow to totally automated systems. We cannot continue analog thinking in a digital world.

The benefits of PDF printing and publishing are most evident in a systems environment. Today, our perception of a system is a bunch of Macs and/or PCs cabled together to share various output devices. In reality, the network configuration and functionality are the most important issues in pre-press and pre-publishing productivity.

Before Networks

When computers were first introduced they were batch-processing oriented. All work was delivered to the computer for processing en masse. By the 1970s, typewriter and then video terminals were attached to the computer to provide access to files and CPU processing. This gave users increasing amounts of interactivity. There were limitations to the number of terminals that could be connected and users were limited in what they could do and when they could do it. This led to the development of local area networks as an alternative method of connecting people and computers.

Network Basics

A network is everything that ties computers together and enables them to communicate, including hardware and cables (the physical things) and software (the stuff you can't see but makes it all work). A network allows computers to be connected together, so that they may share common software, data, or devices. A network is the sum of all its parts.

Computers may be connected in many different ways. Apple Macintosh computers may be connected using either LocalTalk or Ethernet. Windows-based PCs and compatible computers are typically connected using Ethernet. LocalTalk and Ethernet describe the physical aspects of connecting computers and additional software is needed to make the system operate.

Networking Macintosh computers

In the Macintosh environment, this software is included—AppleTalk. In the Windows environment, it is necessary to add additional software such as Microsoft Windows for Workgroups, Artisoft Lantastic, Novell NetWare, or others. Microsoft Windows 95 network software is built-in.

In the Macintosh environment, the simplest and least expensive network approach is LocalTalk, which is built into every Macintosh.

You can construct a simple network of two Macintosh computers using LocalTalk with PhoneNet-compatible connectors— common telephone wire that connects computers, and the same wire that is used to connect a telephone to the wall jack. You can also use the same connectors to connect computers to your printer and share it.

A LocalTalk-based network can be as simple as two computers and a printer connected together. With LocalTalk, computers and printers may be over a thousand feet apart, depending on the quality of the cable used. Computers are strung together, or daisy chained, using the connectors. If additional computers or printers need to be added to the network, they can be daisy chained into the existing connections.

This type of connection is inexpensive, but not very fast. The speed of the communication between computers is 230,400 bits per second. This may seem fast when compared to the fastest modems available, but it may not be fast enough.

An alternative is to use Ethernet, a much faster networking technology—at least 43 times faster than LocalTalk. 10-Base-T Ethernet is at 10,000,000 bits per second; 100-Base-T is at 100,000,000 bits per second; and 1,000,000,000 bps Ethernet is not far away.

A Macintosh-based network using Ethernet does not connect computers and printers together by daisy chaining them—they are connected into a Hub. A device known as an Ethernet Transceiver is used to connect the cabling to the computer. For the Macintosh to use an Ethernet network, it must have an Ethernet card installed. Most recent Macintosh computers are delivered with a built-in Ethernet card. Most computer stores or catalogs can supply the card and instructions for installing it. The Ethernet Transceiver connects the card in your computer to the cabling of the network. The maximum distance supported by Ethernet is 500 meters.

Once the Ethernet network is physically set up, the Network Control Panel in the Macintosh is used to select Ethernet rather than built-in LocalTalk. With Ethernet in place, the only difference the user will notice is improved performance. One of the computers on the network is designated as the Server, and the other computers are Clients. Usually, the fastest computer should be the Server.

Networking Windows Computers

The networking picture in the Windows environment is more

Bits per second
Kbps = kilo (thousands) of bits per second
Mbps = mega (millions) of bits per second

230,400 bps would be 230.4 Kbps.

Usually if the number is even thousand or millions we use kbps or mbps but if it is not, the whole number is presented.

Computer modems are now about 28.8 Kbps or 28,800 bps. They started out at 300 bps — honest!

Most printers for Apple computers are not directly compatible with Ethernet, so the use of a LocalTalk-to-Ethernet gateway is needed. The gateway converts the high speed Ethernet communications to the lower speed LocalTalk format so that existing printers can understand the information. Some high end printers, imagesetters and platemakers will directly support Ethernet without a gateway.

Two cabling types in use: 10-Base-T and 100-Base-T. The number comes from the speed of the network (10 or 100 megabits per second), "Base" refers to the communications technology (Baseband), and the "T" refers to Twisted Pair, the actual physical cabling type. Devices in a 10-Base-T network must be within 100 meters of one another.

Bits galore
Bit = 0 or 1

Byte = 8 bits

Kilobyte ≈ 1,000 (thousand) bytes
or 8,000 bits

Megabyte ≈ 1,000,000 (million)
bytes or 8,000,000 bits

Gigabyte ≈ 1,000,000,000 (billion)
bytes or 8,000,000,000

Terrabyte ≈ 1,000,000,000,000 (tril-
lion) bytes or 8,000,000,000,000

Humungabyte ≈ A Whopper with
large fries.

complex. The physical aspects of networking are almost the same as the Macintosh environment but LocalTalk is not used in the Windows environment. The networking method built into Windows for Workgroups or Windows 95 is known as the Microsoft Windows Network. This method is similar to AppleTalk in appearance and operation. The printer is connected directly to a computer, rather than to the hub itself. In the PC environment, the computer allows its directly connected printer to be shared. Any computer on the network can then connect to the shared printer and print. Most Ethernet cards for PCs come with a connection on the card, so a transceiver is not needed. Certain newer Macintoshes are also configured this way.

AppleTalk and the Microsoft Windows Network are known as peer-to-peer networks. This means that any computer can be a Server, and any computer can be a Client. A computer can also be a Server to one computer and a Client to another at the same time.

Local Area Networks
A local area network (LAN) is a collection of hardware, software and users brought together so as to allow them to cooperate in a fully integrated environment. A LAN typically covers a limited geographical area, measured in meters rather than in kilometers. LANs can cover the linking of two to several hundred users spanning a single office, to one or more departments spanning several floors of a building or spanning an entire site. LANs usually complement Wide Area Networks (WANs) to extend this environment to interconnect or bridge LANs locally or across great distances to form larger networks. LANs encompass:
- Computers
- Workstations
- Peripherals, such as printers and fixed disks
- Cabling and associated components
- Software

Interconnection
There are three techniques for the interconnection of computer equipment:
- *Centralized:* The system is a self contained entity capable

of autonomous operation. The units of communication in such cases are Address and Data Blocks and work in a Master-Slave Relationship. A standalone mainframe is a prime example.

- *Decentralized:* This is communication between systems. The units of communication in this case are Byte and Data Blocks and work in a Master-Slave Relationship. A mainframe computer with Concentrator(s) attached to it falls in this category.
- *Distributed:* This is network communication among self contained autonomous intelligent systems. Such a system works in a relationship of Co-operation and not Master-Slave. A cluster of Macintoshes connected to a cluster of Sun workstations connected to a cluster of PCs is a good example of such a system. LANs fall in the category of Distributed Systems.

Sharing of Information and Resources

A distributed system should look transparent to the user. The whole system should appear as one large dedicated local system and all the remote resources should appear as if they were local to the user. The interface to such a system should be simple and user friendly. People usually work in groups, and perform related tasks. Whatever information is presented on paper can also travel over a LAN in the form of data. This ability to transfer data throughout a department or an organization enables users to exchange messages, documents, forms and graphic files. They also have access to common software packages on the LAN. Though information itself is a resource, the primary purpose of installing a LAN is to share system resources, like the ability to share software and peripherals such as laser printers, optical disks, etc.

Disadvantages of a LAN

The disadvantages of a LAN are:

- General administration, backing up, adding new users, loading software, etc., have to be done by a competent person or staff, called the Network Administrator.
- If the file server fails in the middle of a session, sometimes it is not possible to salvage all user files, as some Servers do not provide for incremental back ups.

In a properly administered network, data stored on the file server would be regularly backed up and this would take the pain out of backing up files from the users point of view. Also, the file server itself can be kept in a physically secure room, which means better security, particularly for sensitive customer data.

- Security of Data: If the file server is not in a reasonably secure place, then unauthorized people may gain access. If user privileges and file protection mechanisms are not properly implemented, it becomes open to misuse.

LAN Concepts

The first component of a LAN is the Communication Channel, also called the transmission or the LAN medium, and typically should have the following characteristics:

- High speed bandwidth
- Flexible and extendible
- Reliable and maintainable

A LAN medium defines the nature of the physical path along which the data must travel, and allows a great number and wide variety of hardware devices to exchange large amounts of information at high speed over limited distances.

LAN Topologies

The physical medium may be arranged in a number of ways. The overall geometric shape, or Topology, is very important in a LAN design. There are three basic practical topologies used in LANs: Star, Ring, and Bus.

Star Networks

This topology usually forms the basis of a wide area network. In this type of network, each station is connected to a central switch by a dedicated physical link. The switch provides a path between any two devices wishing to communicate either physically in a circuit switch or logically in a packet switch.

Ring Networks

Stations are connected by a loop of cable and each connection point, called a Repeater, is responsible for passing on each fragment of the data. Access is not under central control and the data is sent in packets. Within each station, there is a controller board which is responsible for:

- Recognizing packets addressed to that workstation
- Controlling access to the ring—deciding when it is clear to start transmitting.

Transceiver
To connect your network cable to a computer, you need an adapter. The transceiver converts the network signal into one that the computer can deal with (and vice versa for data going out from the computer).

Repeater
Network cables can only carry a signal so far before resistance degrades it. A repeater takes the signal at some point, pumps it up, and lets it travel a greater distance.

Hub
A number of computers may be clustered into a section of a network. That section is connected to a hub, which connects to other sections.

Bus Networks

Bus networks are the most common LANs. They do not need any switches, and in their simplest form, no repeaters. They share a common, linear communication medium and each station requires a tap which must be capable of delivering the signal to all the stations on the bus. The data is sent in packets, and each station listens to all transmissions, picking up those addressed to it. Bus networks are passive, since all the active components are in the stations, and a failure affects only that one station. Stations on a Bus network are limited in distance and only one station at a time can transmit.

Choice of a Server

On a network, a Server is a computer with a large amount of disk storage that has shared software and information. Other computers on the network are Clients and access the software or information as needed on the Server. Choosing the right server and equipping it properly are the keys to the success of a LAN. A server is usually a computer that holds bulk of the LAN Operating System and shares its resources with workstations. In most LANs, a single Server:

- Stores shared files
- Stores software
- Links to printers or other output devices
- Links to tape drives and storage media
- Links to modems
- Links to RIPs

These resources are shared by all connected users. As a LAN grows, these functions are spread over many servers and separate data management and communication servers may be needed.

One of the first decisions is whether to buy:

- a standard PC or Macintosh as a dedicated server and tailor it with third party add-ons.
- a PC or Mac designed as a proprietary server unit.
- a Sun Computer or Silicon Graphics workstation as a server.

As a rule of thumb, plan on 1 Tbyte of Server storage or at least 500 Gbytes.

You can boost performance further by using a disk controller that also incorporates a dedicated cache of high speed RAM.

Typically, a LAN outgrows a server at about 40 users, but the limit depends on the applications in use. A server can be used either as a Dedicated Server or as a Concurrent Server. Using the server as a Concurrent Server degrades network performance, and may even crash the network — so forget it.

Dedicated Server

Networking methodologies use a Dedicated Server. In this case, one computer (typically a very fast one) is designated as a Dedicated Server. All other computers that attach to it are Clients only. This technique is used for larger networks that demand higher performance than can be realized with peer-to-peer networks.

With a Dedicated Server, all shared files are on the Server, and the Client computers access it for their information. A Server will usually have a network operating system installed on it (Novell, Lantastic, etc.) and the monitor and keyboard will be removed. The Server will automatically start its software on power up, and only service requests from the network. Printing is shared as before, except that in very large networks, another computer is usually designated as a Print Server, and will only service printing needs.

Proprietary Servers

Because proprietary Server options are designed for a particular LAN operating system, you avoid incompatibilities that crop up with a standard PC. For example, some third party back-up systems and power supplies do not work reliably with certain LAN Operating Systems. Proprietary units are optimized for their specific LAN Operating System.

Storage

A fast hard disk and disk controller are vital to server's performance. A disk with 40 ms average seek time is too slow for most LANs. If you expect a lot of traffic, consider a 16 ms or less system. How much storage you will need depends on applications. If you want to store a lot of shared files and programs on the server, think big. Get a disk controller that can daisy chain several drives together, so you can add storage as needed. You will certainly need more drives, if you plan to use the disk mirroring options available with LAN operating systems as a backup approach..

ms= millisecond

A measure of disk access time. For instance, the amount of time from when data is requested by the CPU to when the drive returns the data.

Cache RAM

The more memory available for a server's hard disk, the faster the server, and LAN operating system will run. Think big again—say 100 MB of RAM. Since fetching data from the cache is much quicker than getting it from disk, disk caching can speed access to hard disk data. It stores the last data read from the drive plus the next few sectors in RAM, gambling that the software will request that data next.

Network Adapter Cards
No matter how fast the Server, performance is limited by the speed of the Server's LAN adapter card. Most vendors offer intelligent cards, equipped with RAM to speed throughput, but they are a bit more expensive.

CPU
Make sure the Server uses a CPU with the fewest wait states. Zero is the best, and two are too many. If the network is really busy, use a server with a 100 MHz CPU or better.

Back-up
A Server should preferably be equipped with a tape back-up unit that can hold all the files you want to store. The backup software should be compatible with your LAN operating system, and should be capable of backing up all system files. It should also be capable of running while the Server is on-line, and perform while unattended.

Drivers
One adapter card will exchange packets over a shared cable with any other adapter, since they all conform to the same electrical signalling, physical connection and media access specifications. But things are different on the software side of the card. Since each manufacturer designed and implemented its adapter using slightly different hardware components, each adapter needs customized software in order to address them and to move data through the system. This piece of software is known as the driver software.

Print Servers
A Print Server receives jobs from a user on a network, stores that job in a queue, and then forwards the job to an output device on the network—most networks have multiple output devices, from low-res laser printers to a high-res imagesetters and

platemakers. Features such as queue management, statistics reporting, printer setup, and file storage for later printing are usually common. A typical scenario:

- Select *Print* from the application's menu.
- Your computer connects to the printer and asks if it is ready to accept a job.
- If the printer is busy with another job, the computer waits for the printer which may only need to finish somebody else's job or you may be the seventh person waiting to print.
- When the printer is ready, the computer sends the first packets of data which the printer receives and processes (while your computer waits) until the job has been completely sent to the printer.

If you're the ninth person waiting to print, the wait could be enormous. (You might show your college ID when you enter the queue and get a senior citizen discount before your computer is freed for use again.)

Most computers allow you to print in the background. Background printing means that when you select Print, the computer saves the job to a file and a separate piece of software handles getting that file to the printer, when the printer becomes available. You can continue working on the computer while the job prints. When the computer needs to send data to the printer, the application running in the foreground may have to pause, tying up your computer. In addition to releasing your workstation faster, a print server should also be able to:

- Manage multiple print queues
- Set up the printer
- Produce status reports

Queue Management

A print queue is a series of jobs waiting to print. A Print Server usually manages multiple queues, either for the same printer or for different printers. When combined with the set up feature, a Print Server can have different queues for a single output, each with an individual setup. The Print Server usually has different types of queues:

- Active—jobs print when the output device is available

- Hold—jobs print when the administrator releases them
- Completed—printed jobs remain stored on disk for archiving or reprinting
- Error—jobs that could not print for any reason are stored for review

The active queue is used when you have a job to print and you want to print it now. You can use a hold queue, for example, if you want to print jobs overnight. That way, jobs that need to get out during the day get sent to the active queue, and jobs waiting in the hold queue get sent when network load is lower, or when higher-priority jobs have finished printing. A completed queue lets you hold onto jobs for future printing; and an error queue holds the jobs that could not print because of either a printer error, a PostScript error, or a network error. Then, you can fix the error and resend the job. The hold queue, in particular, lets you manage the printing services on your network. Jobs can be sent to the print server computer, but don't print until the system administrator directs them to the appropriate active queue. This type of queue works for jobs requiring special attention, such as special media (film or plate) or switch settings. They can be held until the system administrator has the output device set up properly.

The ability to support multiple print queues allows you to designate queues for specific print devices, so you automate job routing and eliminate manual switching. For instance, you can have a queue for a plain-paper device and one for a film device. During the proofing stages of the job you send it to the plain-paper queue; for the final pass you send it to the film device. To manage all these queues, the Print Server should be able to:
- delete jobs in a queue
- redirect jobs from one queue to another
- change priority of jobs in an output queue
- view the status of jobs in the queue
- enable or disable any of the queues

In addition to managing the jobs within the queues, the Print Server should let you tie specific printer options to a queue. If you have a high-res imagesetter, you might want to have different queues for low, medium, and high resolutions, depending on the job's requirements. Then, you only need to select the queue that is called "2400 dpi film" for example, and the job automatically goes to the correct output device and prints at the correct resolution. For plain-paper laser printers, you could have different queues for the different paper trays. For digital color presses like the Agfa Chromapress you could have multiple devices with certain types of paper in use.

By including a printer configuration in the print queue, jobs always print the way you want them to print. For an imagesetter, you can use printer setups to make sure all the RIP settings are set correctly. Settings such as page orientation, negative or mirror image modes, resolution selection, and page grouping can be set by the Print Server before a job is sent to the imagesetter. A Print Server should be able to set any of the options available from the RIP's software.

The Print Server also maintains statistics about each job, providing the user with a report on printing times, number of pages printed, source workstation name, date and time of job, and more. This report could be in a format that can be imported into IBM Lotus, Microsoft Excel, or other programs for billing or accounting. Prepress service bureaus charge by the minute for jobs that exceed expected runtimes and a Print Server's job log provides the exact runtime for each job.

OPI Servers

High resolution scanned images are the largest consumers of disk space, processing time, and transmission time in a printing and publishing network. While larger disks, data compression, faster computers, and faster networks help to carry the load, better management of graphics data is one of the best ways to improve any system's performance.

Benefits of OPI
- *Higher prepress productivity.*
- *Fast workstation release lets you get back to work in seconds rather than minutes.*
- *High-speed fetches to the Server result in more efficient network usage.*
- *Efficient system management.*

When the image requires color correction, retouching, or special effects, it belongs at the workstation. When the image has been approved for use, it belongs either on a Server or at the RIP. When the job is run, the system should be able to locate the image without tying up anybody's workstation. OPI lets you configure an efficient production cycle by performing tasks at appropriate locations on the network.

Color Separation Houses

Color separations are the largest files encountered in electronic prepress. When you add up all four separations, you could have files totalling 60 megabytes or more. Files of this size can impair productivity unless they are managed correctly. In color separation houses, OPI does just that:

1. Scan images into a color workstation.
2. Touch up images on that workstation, or move them to a workstation dedicated to image editing.
3. Make color separations and transfer them to the OPI Server. For network efficiency, you can transfer the images to the server in a batch during periods of low network traffic or via "sneaker-net" on appropriate media:
   - Tape cartridges
   - Zip or Jaz disks
   - SyQuest disks
   - Magneto optical discs
   - CD-ROM discs

You can use the network or any file sharing utility, or transportable disk to transfer the high-resolution file to or from the Image Server. Once you make a callout to a high-res file, do not move it or change its name. If you do, the OPI function cannot locate it to include in a job.

With the separations resident on the Server, the output device can be fed a continuous stream of image data. At the same time, the workstations are freed of data transmission burdens and used as intended: page design, image retouching and separation. In this way, OPI allows color separation and outputting to run in parallel, with no time wasted for data transmission.

Prepress Service Bureaus

Service bureaus benefit from the same production flow as color separators. Service bureaus send not only color separations through their imagesetters, but also lots of monochrome pages or text pages that contain color images. The workstation operators making up the pages use only low-res EPS or TIFF callouts, so their layout files are easily managed. When they send the job to the imagesetter, their workstations release quickly and they can begin working on the next job.

After they have scanned and stored the high-res images, they can return only the preview file to customers. Customers can work with the preview file in their page layout program, and crop, scale, rotate, or any other manipulations. The preview file is generally small enough to be sent on diskettes or E-mail.

Newspapers

Newspapers use different production systems to create different types of work with one system for editorial text, another for charts and illustrations, and another for display ads. A single newspaper page may contain elements from all these systems. At deadline time, when the last element required for a page is approved, the page must be printed as fast as possible. Printing complex broadsheet pages containing many images without an OPI solution ties up a page layout station. OPI allows the storage of graphics in a central location on the network, so users can access them with low-res callouts.

Magazines

Magazines, like newspapers, use different production systems to create different types of work with systems for editorial text, charts and illustrations, and display ads. OPI enables the integration of these separate files at the output device. Magazine production operations accrue the same benefits as newspapers for display ad work, and many of the same benefits as a color house for color separations. For display ads, magazines have logos and clip art that are used repeatedly by advertisers. In addition, magazines use photos, graphics, and icons for section identifiers. Typical magazine color uses a 133-line screen. Higher line screens means scanning at higher resolutions, resulting in larger file sizes. When a magazine brings their production work inhouse, they set up a color production cycle similar to a color separators'.

Data management is now probably the biggest hurdle publications need to address. For a single publication produced direct to plate, there are huge volumes of data. Each full-page ad scanned on a copy dot scanner requires 180 MB of storage (45 MB for each single-color separation). The data management situation for ads is complicated by the requirement to handle scheduling, versioning and sometimes split runs. There are composite editorial pages, which include low-resolution FPO view files and associated high-resolution scans of editorial images. Storage, both live and archival, becomes a major issue, as does management and tracking. In order to produce 100 of its periodicals using computer-to-plate technology, there will be the need to store and manage 2–2.5 terabytes of information.

Publishers

Because it follows a page model, PDF files are appealing to traditional publishers. One area receiving much attention is the capability to put newsletters or other publications online in PDF form and then have subscribers download the files and read them. To the subscriber, there is the appeal of timely information. To the publisher, there is the appeal of being able to distribute without the overhead of printing. Printers are not thrilled with this idea. This distribution method amounts to a site license to customers to print and distribute copies. Restricting the number of times a customer can download a file does not prevent thousands of copies being sent via E-mail or printed and distributed conventionally by the subscriber, all from a single download.

Image Server

The terms Image Server and OPI Server are used interchangeably but there is an important distinction evolving. Graphic arts firms are storing all images for re-purposing, from print to Web or CD-ROM and back again. These images can be in separate files or part of PDF documents. Since an OPI Server only serves print, the term Image Server may now take on a broader connotation.

An Image Server can be any computer on the network with one or more large disks to store image files, whether they are high resolution for print, or Web screen images or both. You can use one or several computers as Image Servers. The RIP computer must be able to access a disk used to store the high-res graphics.

An efficient way to configure an OPI system is to use the same workstation running the RIP as the Image or Network Server. The high-res image is then transferred to the Server once. At output time, the RIP reads the image from its own disk. No matter how many times the image is output, it only needs to be transferred over the network once. In the real world of production an image is usually used more than once in the publishing process.

The high-resolution images placed on the Image Server will usually be final images with all color correction, retouching, and separation done. If users need to make changes to the high-res image or perform a color correction they can do so if they replace the image on the Image Server with the new image. For such a change, the preview image does not need to be updated. But if a change is made that would affect the way the preview image interacts with the page makeup program, a re-sizing of the image, for example or the way the image is accessed on the Server, like a name or location change, then the preview image must also be regenerated.

If the RIP computer is used as the Image Server, this function only needs to retrieve the high-res image from its own disk. RIP software with OPI functionality is available for Macintosh, Power Macintosh, Sun Computer and Silicon Graphics, and PC/NT computers.

OPI functions may be done at the RIP while some OPI solutions require a free-standing Server for integration. You can configure an OPI system to suit your production needs with:
- Each component on a separate workstation
- RIP and Image Server on the same workstation

When printing to a Print Server (a Server that spools jobs for an output device), the workstation program releases within seconds and the operator goes back to work. Without a spooling capability, the workstation is not released until the job is printed. You send a job containing an OPI callout to the proper queue on the Print Server, and it routes it to the appropriate OPI server for ouput.

One Workflow Model
1. Workstations running OPI-capable application programs place images on the OPI or Image Server over the network.
2. Any workstation on the network sends the job to the appropriate Print Server queue.
3. The Print Server spools the job, releases the workstation, and transmits the job to the appropriate output device.

Transmission time is quick because the job contains only a low-res callout of the image. The RIP with the OPI integrating func-

Servers galore

A *Server* is any device with information shared by Client workstations on a network. Every network must have a Server and it is simply a *Network Server*.

A Network Server stores centralized files that are shared by Clients. It can also be called a *File Server.*

A network could have multiple Servers, one of which could be used to store large image files. It would be called an *Image Server*.

With large volumes of image and data files, some Servers could support a database capability for searching and retrieving the stored data more efficiently. This would make it a *Database Server.*

Another Server common to networks supports a shared printer or other output device. It has its own disk so that jobs are transferred to the disk and the Client workstation does not have to wait until the printer is finished. It is called a *Print Server*. The *Print Server* retains files for future runs or archiving.

All PostScript output systems must have a RIP, a raster image processor. The RIP usually has a large disk to store software and pre- and post-ripped files. It is called a *RIP Server.*

The RIP should be equipped with OPI functionality. The disk and system associated with the RIP is then also called an *OPI Server*.

The Server could encompass multiple functions, such as trapping, imposition and ripping. It might be called a *Super Server.*

Lastly, the Server could fully support Adobe Acrobat 3.0 with its superb collection of high-end printing functions. PDF files can be trapped, imposed and color managed. That gives us a *PDF Server*.

Thus, a network could have all of the above functionality, or some combination, or like most, it could integrate the Server (for the network, image storage, OPI and ripping) and the RIP into one Server. Or the Server into one RIP.

tion reads the callout in the job, and connects to the Images Server as directed. Because the same workstation may be used as the Image Server and the RIP, the integrator only needs to retrieve the image from its disk. The integrator merges the high-res image into the job stream with the other page elements and the page is printed.

Once the publication is output, what happens to the images? In the old days, they were archived to tape. Today, publishers and service firms are interested in the future for their images. That means they want to store in such a way that they can be found quickly, accessed rapidly, and converted to various file formats for print or presentation.

Prepress systems are also tying OPI Servers to image archives. A database becomes important because users cannot find images based only on their file names. Some production pros can retrieve images on this basis, but designers may not. Without reliable image pattern-recognition technology, we have to rely on keywords, indexed fields and full-text queries of captions or description files. These are typically stored in a database (relational or fixed-field) and searched by a full-text indexing engine.

Server Integration
A prepress network usually consists of multiple workstations, a file server and a printer or printers connected by network cables.

Sometimes a print spooler is added so that files destined for the printer are accepted by the spooler to release the workstation's application. The spooler then queues the job or jobs based on prioritization and sends them to the printer. The difference between a print spooler and a print server is based on the amount of time files remain on the disk. A spooler may delete files sooner than a server.

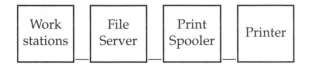

The printer on a prepress network is usually a PostScript-based printer and therefore has a RIP. Most desktop printers have the RIP inside the printer . . .

| RIP | Printer |

. . . while imagesetters and platesetters and proofers have the RIP as a separate unit, connected by a cable. Today, every raster-based output device must have a Raster Image Processor.

| RIP | Printer |

A server may be added to the output function to store ripped files for later printout of the entire file of one or more of the color separations. This may be called a print server or a print spooler. We are going to call it a RIP server because it serves the RIP. At one time there was a RIP for each and every output device. Today, the trend is to try to RIP-once-and-output-many-times. So the RIP server functions as a print spooler/server, holding files for later printout or archiving.

| RIP Server | RIP | Printer |

The RIP server and the RIP may be integrated into one unit.

| RIP Server | RIP | Printer |

An OPI server could be added to the system for automatic picture replacement.

| OPI Server | RIP Server | RIP | Printer |

Or the OPI server and the RIP server could be integrated while the RIP is a separate unit . . .

| OPI Server | RIP Server | RIP | Printer |

. . . or the OPI server, RIP server and RIP could be integrated into one unit.

| OPI Server | RIP Server | RIP | Printer |

At various levels there could be more than one printer, proofer, imagesetter, digital color press, platemaker or other output alternatives.

| OPI Server | RIP Server | RIP | Printers |

When the functions of OPI, RIP and print serve are integrated into one Server, we are going to call it a Super Server. It then is networked with the file server and the printer or printers.

| File Server | Super Server | Printers |

To the Super Server we add the final ingredient of PDF handling, trapping and imposition. The final system now takes form as a *PDF Server*.

Work stations	PDF Server	Multiple Outputs

The Adobe PDF will change the very nature of networks and servers and systems and prepress. With scripts or plug-ins many routine tasks can be automated. For instance, a script might take a QuarkXPress file, open it, distill it, open Acrobat Exchange, perform a function, save it, then serve functions would trap the PDF, impose it based on the electronic work order, direct it to a proofer and prioritize it to a print queue.

Server Schizophrenia: RIPs that trap, impose, serve, and print
OPI Servers, Workflow Servers, Database Servers, File Management and Image Servers. Servers are migrating to ripping and archiving, archive image databases are expanding to handle work in process. Print Servers, once limited to spooling, now perform trapping and imposition and promise to automate workflow, as database-driven workflow software makes similar claims. RIPs once only ripped; now they Serve. Servers only served; now they rip. The result is that almost every Server and almost every RIP system almost do the same thing.

Workflow is changing. Workflow software has migrated from text-based systems to prepress document production that helps route jobs to the required queue or invoke processes when work is dropped in a queue or folder. The Server is simply a central (network) function that can run background tasks like automatic trapping, or rasterizing (ripping) a file for output to a printer, imagesetter, platemaker or whatever. File Servers are based on UNIX or Novell networks, with Macintosh, PC and UNIX workstations handling processing. Workflow may simply mean setting up "hot folders" to perform prepress functions and letting the Super Server do the rest.

The Server approach shifts the processing burden from individual workstations to a central Server for more efficient printing and job handling. Sending files to the Server takes seconds,

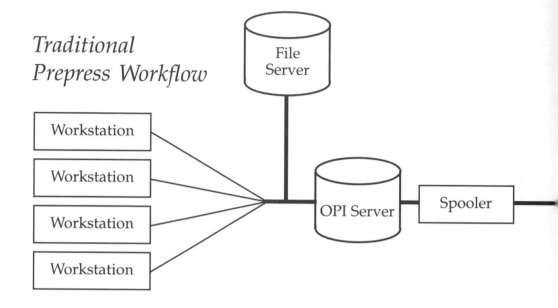

*Traditional
Prepress Workflow*

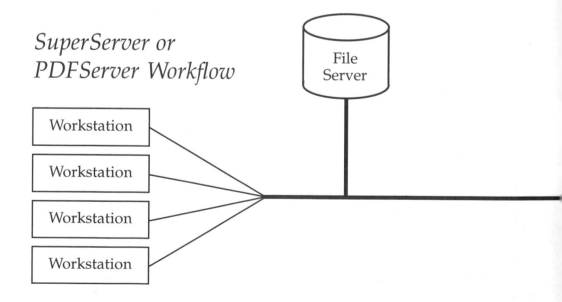

*SuperServer or
PDFServer Workflow*

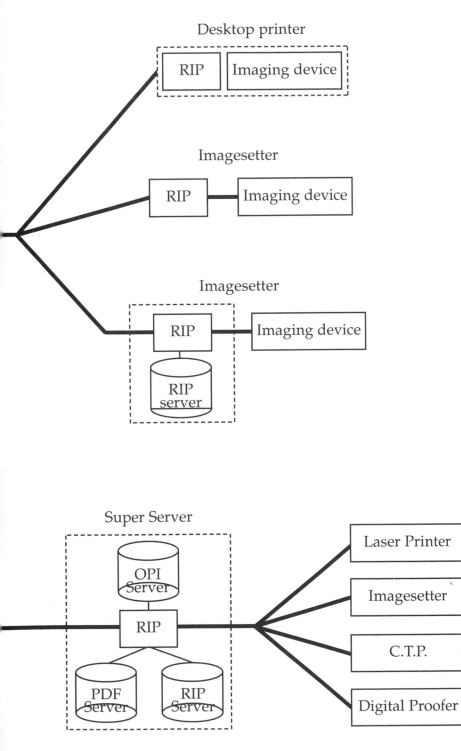

even for pages with gigabytes of images. Software directs where and when each job is to print, inserts high-resolution scans precisely where they belong in the layout, monitors print progress, and maintains statistics. Queued jobs can be rearranged, placed on hold, deleted, or moved among queues with ease. Some Server functions are:

- Unattended management of a number of printers through multiple queues.
- Image substitution through OPI.
- User-definable printer setups.
- Queuing controls.
- Device, application, and platform-independence.
- Control over a job from the server or a workstation.
- Centralized image and print processing.
- Security for printing resources.
- Fast spooling to a central Server.
- Storage and retrieval of images on the network.
- Multiple projects moving and numerous devices working without intervention.
- Accurate replacement and positioning of high-resolution scans before imaging.
- Configure any output device to the resolution, line screen, and screen angle preferred
- Assign multiple queues to the same device, or multiple devices to the same queue.
- Spool PostScript files from any source, output them to any PostScript device.
- Manage files from anywhere on the network, and re-queue without respooling.
- Share images and manage printers through one Server, even if computer types vary.
- Network-based job management
- Enhanced queue monitoring
- Workflow optimization and job load balancing
- PostScript Level 2 or 3 resource management
- Preflight job verification
- Support for in-RIP separation
- Film optimization.
- RIP and output device management
- Integrated RIP
- OPI image replacement.

- Image File Conversion (for PhotoCD, TIFF/IT, CEPS data formats)
- Network connections

Workflow Solutions Aplenty

In 1995 Linotype-Hell pioneered RIP operation, building on the early work done by Monotype with the Lasercomp in the late 1970s. In 1995 the company developed Delta Technology which essentially splits the RIP process into two steps: PostScript interpretation and the object list. PostScript processing takes place in the DeltaWorkstation; screening takes place in the DeltaTower. This whole process is controlled by DeltaSoftware, which includes capabilities such as print spooling and OPI. The DeltaWorkstation is based on Windows NT; its multiprocessing capabilities enable several processors to work in parallel, increasing throughput. The DeltaWorkstation produces the DeltaList, a single layer file identical to what will appear in the final output. The file is transferred to the DeltaTower for screening. The entire system concept allows functions to be handled by separate components: PostScript processing by the DeltaWorkstation, screening by the DeltaTower. All are controlled by DeltaSoftware, including DeltaImage manager and DeltaPrintmanager. A number of vendors have applied Delta technology in their RIP approaches.

Scitex Solutions

The Scitex Brisque RIP system is an output controller for pre-press production. Brisque automates production processes with "job ticket" templates. Each job ticket describes a workflow consisting of operations to be finished in a particular order according to specific parameters. It will not work with non-Scitex output devices, either for final output or proofs (except an HP printer). Brisque supports OPI for the first time on a Scitex device, as well as DCS. It works with CT and New Linework formats, which handle 65,000 unique colors in linework and 32 color channels. It rips data into the internal Scitex CT and linework formats. Both the CT and New Linework formats can be edited. CTs can be edited in Photoshop. Screening is done on the fly by the screening controller built into the Scitex imagesetters. For continuous-tone proofers, the Brisque combines CT and Linework files into a single high-resolution format and will

The RIPs and systems described in this section are only for illustration. It was not our goal to provide a comprehensive review of all available workflows, but rather to provide a sort of overview of some of the products and trends. Those trends which we have observed are:

- *Multi-vendor systems evolving to single-vendor systems*
- *Totally automated workflows — the mouse is in charge*
- *Industry-standard hardware platforms*
- *Industry-standard networking*
- *Integrating RIP functions at multiple stages in the process*
- *The use of the Web as a business tool*

trap CT to LW, LW to CT, and CT to CT. Scitex prefers to rasterize first and work on the rasterized file after. Brisque can drive three different types of output from one RIP.

Cascade Solutions

Cascade Systems' Orion RIP runs under NT or Solaris. It has a workflow control system, plus a connection to Cascade's DataFlow workflow management package. The RIP can be linked to an overall production workflow tracking system that covers total workflow, not just the final output. The key aspect of Cascade's Orion is its Internet browser connectivity through the Orion W3 option. This allows setup, management and monitoring of the overall process from any device on the Internet.

Harlequin Solutions

Harlequin provides workflow management and a facility for editing the data in a "late-binding" fashion that includes trapping. Harlequin has multitasking and multiprocessing but doesn't offer OPI within the RIP, but its OEM customer implementations provide this support. Harlequin also supports a PCI card screening accelerator. Harlequin Display List Technology allows for editability of the PostScript display list, providing a hook for customization between interpretation and rendering. This option lets OEMs and other third party vendors write tailored applications that add customized features to ScriptWorks. Applications include PostScript verification and previewing; object editing; integration of trapping and/or imposition capabilities; conversion from PostScript into other languages or formats like TIFF/IT; the detection and rendering of vignettes using alternative processing; enhanced image processing capabilities. Harlequin is taking advantage of this access to the display list for an integrated automatic RIP-based trapping solution, called EasyTrap.

When the PostScript job draws an object, instead of simply adding the object to the display list and continuing as usual, HDLT will first invoke a procedure. That procedure may be written by an OEM, or a third-party vendor. It can use PostScript to do any computation necessary. Harlequin Display List Technology is available as a layered option for ScriptWorks running on all industry-standard platforms.

AII Solutions

Autologic Information International (AII) has streamlined its RIP capabilities by enabling some key functions to be performed after a job has been rasterized and before it is output to an imaging device. Among these functions are imposition, step-and-repeat processing, proofing and outputting a job multiple times without having to rasterize the file again. This capability, which AII is marketing as Post-RIP Assembly among its commercial customers, is similar to the Bitmap Stitching feature offered to its newspaper customers. For label production and other applications involving step-and-repeat operation, Post-RIP Assembly requires only that an element be rasterized once, after which it can be repeated horizontally and vertically any number of times without re-rasterizing.

For color proofing, AII recombines the rasterized CMYK data and prints them on a color proofer. A software algorithm downsamples the resolution of the raster data for the 300-dpi printer, without having to rasterize again for the different resolution. It is possible also to replace part of a page by substituting one rasterized block for another one based on x, y coordinate positioning. Other post-RIP capabilities include rotating pages 180 degrees and replacing an entire page within an imposed job. The program includes facilities for tracking elements of a publication being output, including reporting where each element resides (with filters available to limit the display to items conforming to certain criteria), which publication and edition each one belongs to, the output device each was sent to, etc. It also provides an error queue for jobs that fail to output and an option to specify how long finished jobs are held before purging.

Rampage Solutions

The Rampage RIPping system is a comprehensive solution for film or plate output. It uses an open-architecture design and lets you connect multiple RIPs to one output device. The RIP runs on industry-standard hardware. Additional productivity features include; automatic trapping, CEPS format support, OPI server functions, imposition, step-and-repeat and Ramproof, a function that allows a ripped file to be output to a proofing device or monitor and then to an imagesetter (RIP once plot twice).

Rampage's TrapIt1 rasterizes an incoming file at low resolution to do its analysis of what kinds of traps are needed, based on the relative luminance values of each pixel. But at the same time, it generates a display list of the objects on the page in drawing order, taking into account the order in which they are layered on top of each other. Traps are then computed for each object relative to the others that are below it in the display list and have intersecting boundaries. The output, new PostScript-like instructions, is generated from the trap decisions and combined with the original PostScript file. Object formats allow layering objects with transparency values, generally impossible in normal PostScript. Another is the ability to select and modify trap areas or other attributes easily because each object is its own element rather than a set of colored pixels. RIP enhancements include:

- Automatic vignette detection, which treats all objects in a vignette as one object at high resolution. Support for gravure output, with antialiasing from high resolution down to gravure resolution, eliminating the need to output film and scan it to accommodate gravure printing.
- Facilities for adjusting press compensation, replacing one set of values with another when switching from a sheetfed press to a web press.
- "Smart shadows," which puts shadows over areas outside a clip path, regardless of what is underneath them.
- "Automatic touchplates" to replace one to four inks each with a different transfer curve of that ink plus add a special spot color with its transfer curve. This works like a duotone to change the curve of one or more of the CMYK inks and add a spot color based on the same data.
- Expansion of blends to 256 elements, regardless of the original input.

Agfa has a distribution agreement with to resell an enhanced version of the Rampage RIPing System. The enhanced version of the Agfa Rampage RIPing System includes Agfa's Balanced Screening. The Agfa Rampage RIPing System includes one or multiple PostScript Level 2 software RIPs, a specialized board for on-the-fly screening, built-in OPI capabilities, and automatic or interactive object-by-object trapping. Rampage generates digital proofs by anti-aliasing the same raster data that will plot on the imagesetter or platesetter. The system can RIP, merge, and plot a variety of file formats, including CT/LW, TIFF, and JPEG, on Agfa imaging systems and digital proofers.

Agfa RIP Solutions

Agfa's Cobra software raster image processor combines a Sun SPARCstation with PostScript Level 2 software RIP. Cobra is based on Adobe's Configurable PostScript Interpreter (CPSI) and is not tied to dedicated RIP hardware in order to migrate to other platforms. Cobra technology offers the synergy of the Sun SPARC processor chips, the advanced Solaris operating system, and the Cobra multi-threaded architecture. Users benefit from improved capabilities of the optional PixelBurst coprocessor. Cobra is also available with optional Agfa CristalRaster stochastic screening and Agfa Balanced Screening Options software to address special halftoning requirements.

Agfa's MultiStar RIP multiplexers are Agfa's solution to the high level of RIP performance needed for intensive production of hi-res TIFF environments. Each MultiStar contains a two-channel RIP multiplexer and can house one to two Emerald-based Star hardware RIPs in one enclosure. Users can combine Agfa hardware and software RIPs for maximum performance and flexibility. A MultiStar-based system can improve the performance of an Agfa imagesetter and RIP by doubling processing capabilities and eliminating RIP bottlenecks.

Agfa's Taipan is a software RIP that provides print spooling functions. With its multithreaded software code, Taipan exploits the multitasking and multiprocessing capabilities of the Windows NT operating system and can be integrated into an existing network of PCs, Macintoshes, and UNIX workstations; and simultaneously accommodates AppleTalk, Hot Folder, TCP/IP and Windows-Named Pipe input channels. Users can benefit from the processing power of Windows NTs, and the flexibility of a PostScript Level 2 software RIP. Taipan can be updated with a software upgrade.

Agfa's Viper software RIP brings enhanced color management of Adobe PostScript Level 2 to Macintosh-based design and production environments. Viper is also based on Adobe's Con-

Many suppliers have provided RIP systems that maximize off-the-shelf workstations. Thus, Agfa, for example, has software RIPs for Sun, Mac, PC/NT and other computer hardware platforms.

Job Tickets are just the ticket
Agfa Mainstream is Workflow Server software that runs on Sun workstations and handles the queueing and job management of all jobs in process. It has some extra features such as load balancing, preflight, filmsaving, and more. It can also automate trapping and imposition using standard desktop applications such as TrapWise and Presswise. It uses the concept of "hot folders."

This concept came from a need for:
- *the need to define and indicate upfront the steps the job had to go through*
- *the need to have the full "processing" information available at any moment by anyone involved in completing the process*
- *the need to control and "post calculate" a job*

Improvements in workflow and automation of the communication between production processes are crucial success factors. Until today the choice for prepress automation has been:

- *the closed system approach with proprietary "big file" data formats including a proprietary workflow approach*
- *the open PostScript system, based on separate components — each the very best available for their specific functionality — but also with unpredictable production performance and an incremental step-by-step workflow approach.*

figurable PostScript Interpreter (CPSI) software for imagesetters, and Adobe's PixelBurst coprocessor. Viper runs on a standard Mac platform and as a software RIP, it can migrate to more powerful Macintosh platforms.

Adobe Solutions

Once again, Adobe has met the demands of changing communication technology by creating a RIP architecture for production printing systems. The main goal of Supra is to produce high performance, large production capacity, with a quick turnaround. In order to satisfy personalized printing expectations, Supra must be able to handle large amounts of variable information for each different page, and it must be able to produce reliably and predictably. Adobe is currently working with OEMs to reach these goals.

Supra is a RIP technology which can process both PostScript and PDF streams. Files first enter the "Coordinator" which determines whether the file is PS or PDF by its inherent page independence. The PS files go to the "Normalizer" and the PDF files go to the "Page Store." The "Normalizer" acts as Acrobat's Distiller and converts the PS file to a PDF. These distilled files

Adobe Supra Architecture

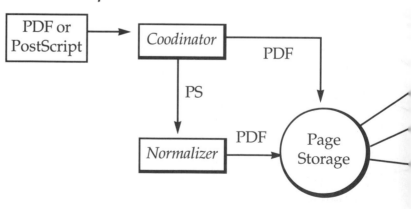

then continue on to the "Page Store" where all documents are stored as PDFs. Pages are processed through the RIP and finally passed on to the "Assembler" which dictates the flow of information to the marking engine. In addition to digital presses, Supra's technology is applicable to large-format imagesetters, proofers, and platemakers.

PostScript is a standard, and it is supported by the majority of RIPs. PDF is an almost perfect format for a RIP system due to its compressed size. Preflighting and proofing are streamlined as well, due to decreased transmission time. Redos are also simplified and less costly due to the editability of PDF.

Agfa PDF Workflow

In 1997, Agfa Division of Bayer advanced RIP and Server architecture to a higher level by establishing the Acrobat 3.0 PDF as the standard for moving document files around a prepress network. Agfa designed a digital workflow that re-engineers preflight checking, automated job tickets, automatic picture replacement, soft proofing, trapping, queuing, imposition, screening and rasterization.

Predictable in file integrity.
Missing fonts or PostScript resources used to mean long coffee breaks. In "high-end" PDF, all the font information is included in the file. No more need to have all the fonts available by all the players in the production process.

Predictable in processing time.
In a modern workflow you want to predict the time it will take to process a file. When your digital platemaker has to supply printing plates for a press, you have to have a good idea how long it will take to produce your plates. Press downtime costs a small fortune. In a busy service bureau, you need to know how long a file will RIP so you can deliver it yesterday.

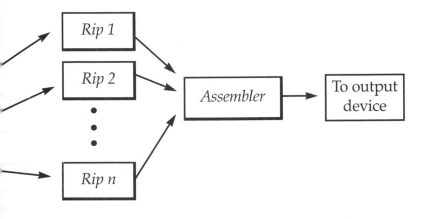

The high-end PDF format is very flexible

Flexible as in editable, easy to repurpose, and accessible. As we phase from "pre-press to pre-media" designers and publishers want to be able to reuse or repurpose the created content in different media: digital proofing, multimedia CD-ROM, Intranet and Web publishing.

Where in PostScript the procedures, variables and controls are performed on a document basis, the PDF format allows to do all activity on the individual pages. That is very important in environments where different documents or pages of documents have to be handled differently, such as when imposition of specific pages or last minute corrections need to be done.

The high-end PDF format allows all of this in a convenient way . . .

. . . because it is page-independent and ready to use across platforms, operating systems, software applications and output devices and, hence, is ideal for repurposing of information. It is built with Acrobat plug-in mechanisms to handle issues and edit the file right down to the page level in every step of the production process.

The new workflow from Agfa is the first to exploit the features of Acrobat 3.0 PDF. It applies Supra as its print architecture which applies the page-independent and predictable nature of the PDF to its fullest.

The PDF now permits "blind transfers"—communication of jobs on a more reliable basis. Like the Italian sauce commercial, a PDF has "everything in it." Fonts and files will no longer be among the missing. The very nature of preflight will change . . . for the better.

In this approach, the PDF which has been distilled into the list of page objects only requires rasterizing in order to actually print out. Thus a Supra RIP is essentially a rasterizer. Thus, jobs are divided into pages, processed, and sent to individual rasterizers. This parallel processing makes workflow much more efficient.

As a result, jobs can flow through the system, being trapped, imposed, and more. For instance, imposition is better done with the PDF than with a bitmap file and bottling is the best example.

The network now allows every user to view and access jobs. But the real power of this workflow comes from the automated job ticket approach. Almost every aspect of production is now a part of the file and directs its own destiny to any printout device or function.

CHAPTER 5

CREATING PDF FILES

Creating a PDF

The first step in any information distribution system is the determination of how the document will be used and who will use it. An end-use evaluation for the PDF focuses on distribution and usage concerns. How will the PDF be distributed and used? If the intended distribution is Web-based and on-screen viewing, then portability and small file size are important. However, if the end use is high-end output to an imagesetter or platesetter, then image integrity becomes the overriding factor. An analogy is that of a scale. On one side of the scale is image integrity and on the other side is file compression.

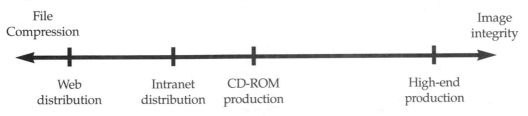

Currently there are two ways (actually 2.5 ways) to create PDF files—PDFWriter and Acrobat Distiller. Depending on end-use, one or the other will best suit your needs. The choice is actually very simple. When producing text documents with small amounts of graphics that are not intended to be printed for professional production purposes, PDFWriter is a good choice. If high-end production is the goal and proper reproduction of graphics is essential, then use Distiller. The growing repurposability of documents and intense needs of high-end printing requires the use of Distiller.

PDF Writer is found in the Macintosh Chooser as a special printer driver.

Acrobat PDFWriter
The PDFWriter appears as a printer choice in the Chooser. PDF files are created by accessing the Page Setup and Print dialog boxes of the document creating application.

Compared to regular printer drivers, there are two buttons in the Page Setup dialog box that are special for PDFWriter, Compression and Fonts. With these functions the user can control how the PDF file will be created.

Compatibility
There are different base compression schemes used by Acrobat 2.1 and 3.0. Acrobat 2.1 base compression is LZW and Acrobat 3.0 uses a ZIP-like base compression. ZIP compression is approximately 20% more effective than LZW. Acrobat 3.0 compatibility also preserves halftone information which used to be discarded by Acrobat 2.1. Acrobat 3.0 also compresses fonts more efficiently than 2.1.

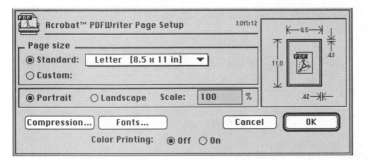

Compared to regular printer drivers, there are two buttons in the "Page Setup" dialog box that are special for PDF Writer, compression and fonts. With these functions the user can control how the PDF file will be saved.

To ensure that your PDF document can be read by everyone, Acrobat 2.1 compatibility is a safe choice. However, if you'd like the added benefits of ZIP compression, use Acrobat 3.0 compatibility. This also makes sense because the Acrobat 3.0 Reader is available for free download at www.adobe.com.

ASCII Format vs. Binary Format
PDFWriter's default setting is binary which makes the PDF file approximately 20% smaller than saving them in ASCII format.

Compression
The most common reason for generating a PDF file is to enhance its transportation capabilities on digital media, either over a network or on storage devices. File size is often critical in order to best utilize storage space. Both PDFWriter and Distiller offer several types of compression which fall into two main categories, *lossy* and *lossless*.

Lossy Compression
The compression technique most used for contone images is called Joint Photographic Experts Group (JPEG). JPEG falls into the category of lossy compression methods. This sounds worse than it actually is. Even though some information is taken away from the image to reduce the file size, the lost information is such that is not detectable in the image. There are five JPEG compression options:
- *High compression*
- *Medium-high compression*
- *Medium compression*
- *Medium-low compression*
- *Low compression*

No compression. Distilling time 85 seconds.
File size 3870 K Compression ratio: 1

Low JPEG compression. Distilling time 86 seconds.
File size 1802 K. Compression ratio: 2.14

Low-medium JPEG compression. Distilling time 81 seconds.
File size 1321 K. Compression ratio: 2.9

Medium JPEG compression. Distilling time 77 seconds.
File size 775 K. Compression ratio: 5.0

Medium-high JPEG compression. Distilling time 85 seconds.
File size 524 K. Compression ratio: 7.4

High JPEG compression. Distilling time 74 seconds.
File size 394 K. Compression ratio: 9.8

The compression dialog box for PDF Writer lets the user choose between the amount of JPEG compression or if a lossless method should be used.

Remember the balanced scale analogy on page 77? JPEG compression options are not the same as in Photoshop. Acrobat's "High" setting refers to compression and Photoshop's "Maximum" JPEG setting refers to image quality.

JPEG-High yields high compression rates with noticeable loss in image quality while *JPEG-Low* compresses little but preserves image quality. PDFWriter's default setting for JPEG compression is *Medium* which results in acceptable image quality for most images, depending on what you consider acceptable to be. To see the differences, look at the comparison on the previous pages.

The compression ratio is not the same for each picture. It depends on the amount of compressible data. Images with smooth changes between tones will be compressed more than images with sharp edges and large changes in color and lightness. The JPEG algorithm is designed to compress continuous tone images, like photos. JPEG is not the best choice for compressing images with sharp changes in tone like screen captures or computer-generated line drawings.

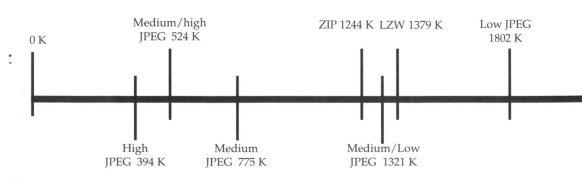

Lossless Compression

Lossless compression schemes do not suffer the same data loss that JPEG compression does. LZW/ZIP, CCITT Groups 3 & 4 and Run Length Encoded (RLE) are all lossless compressions.

Only LZW/ZIP can compress color, grayscale and monochrome images. The Compatibility setting (Acrobat 2.1 or 3.0) will determine whether LZW or ZIP compression will be used. LZW/ZIP works well on the color/grayscale images with sharp changes in tone like the screen captures in this book.

Monochrome Compression

The final type of lossless compression offered by PDFWriter is for *Monochrome Bitmap Images*. The four compression techniques are:
- *CCITT Group 3*
- *CCITT Group 4*
- *LZW/ZIP*
- *RLE*

The basic compression idea of these methods is that if a picture has 5000 pixels of black in a row, the file does not define the color of each pixel. For example, *pixel 1 is black, pixel 2 is black, pixel 3 is black, . . . pixel 4999 is black and pixel 5000 is black.* Rather it is defined as: *the following 5000 pixels are black.* In PDFWriter this compression scheme is also used for text.

A visual comparison between the different compression rates that was accomplished on the picture on the proceeding pages

Without compression
3870 K

*Uncompressed
TIFF file*

File size: 377 K
Compression ratio: 1

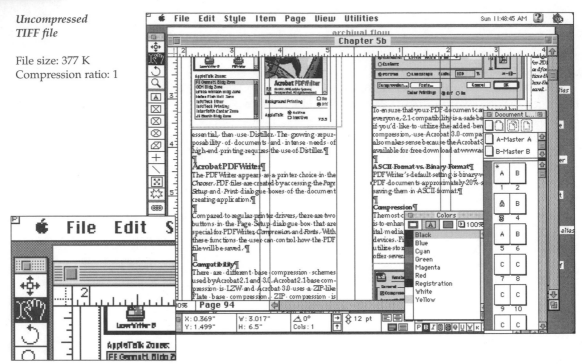

*Low JPEG
compression*

File size: 259 K
Compression ratio: 1.45

Note the noise in the
white areas. This is due
to the compression tech-
niques used in JPEG.

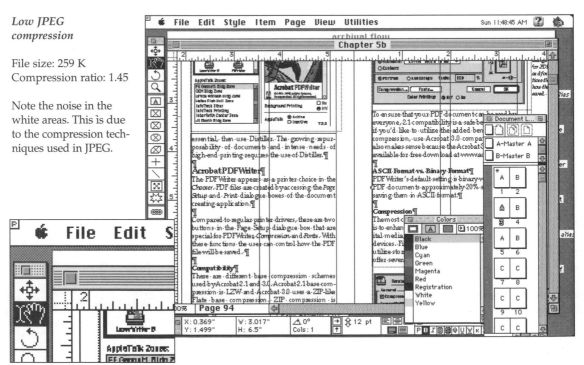

Medium JPEG compression

File size: 166 K
Compression ratio: 2.27

The compression is higher but the noise is becoming more noticeable.

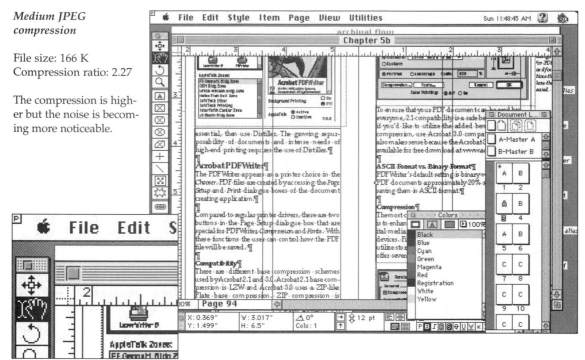

High JPEG compression

File size: 120 K
Compression ratio: 3.16

The compression is much lower than the what was achieved in the images on page 80-85. And the noise now make the whole background gray.

ZIP 4 bit compression

File size: 28 K
Compression ratio: 13.6

As ZIP is a lossless compression algorithm, the quality is the same as in the original, and because the compression scheme is optimal for line art and artificial pictures the compression is very high.

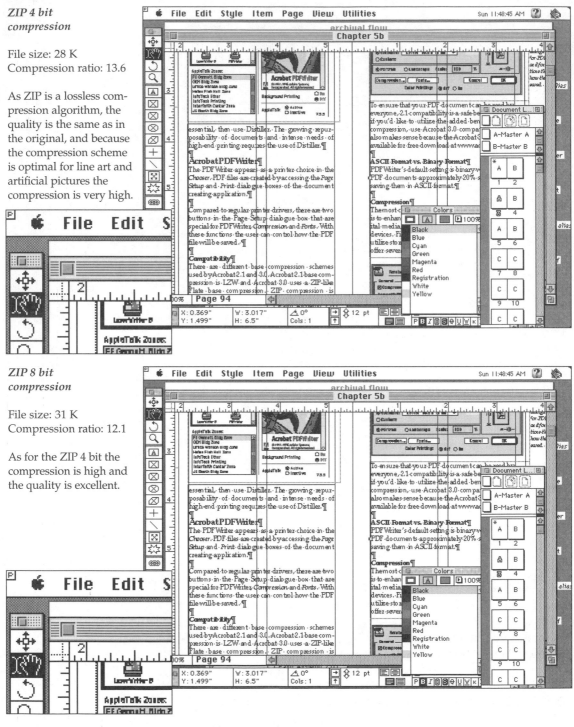

ZIP 8 bit compression

File size: 31 K
Compression ratio: 12.1

As for the ZIP 4 bit the compression is high and the quality is excellent.

The font embedding samples on page 94–95 were scanned and compressed using the above methods. The resulting sizes were:

Original File	*4.7 MB*
CCITT Group 4	*87 times smaller*
ZIP	*41 times smaller*
LZW	*32 times smaller*
CCITT Group 3	*29 times smaller*
RLE	*13 times smaller*

Downsampling Images

Downsampling reduces the resolution of images within a document. This results in smaller PDF file size. If the *Downsample Images* box is checked, PDFWriter will reduce the resolution of all monochrome, grayscale and color images with the nearest integral factor that will result in a resolution as close as possible to 72 dpi. For instance, a 300 dpi image would be downsampled to 75 dpi—reducing the image file size by a factor of 16. Why downsample to 72 dpi? Because PDFWriter should be used primarily to produce PDFs for on-screen viewing and since most monitors are 72–96 dpi devices.

Font Embedding

The marvel of Acrobat is its ability to retain all document font information—kerning, character shape and scaling—while keeping the formatted information in a semi-editable text format. This is essential to maintain the look and feel of the document. PDFWriter can embed the fonts used in a document to ensure that the required font data is present when the document is displayed or printed on another computer which may not have the particular fonts installed. The receiving computer may not even use the same font format (Mac vs. PC fonts).

PDFWriter handles font inclusion in two different ways:
1. Embeds the entire font or a subset of the font.
2. Uses substitute fonts based on original font metrics and style.

Embedding Fonts

If selected in *Font* options in the Page Setup window, PDFWriter will embed the fonts used in the original document in the resulting PDF document. Each font embedded will be approximately 20K in the final PDF file size. In order to keep PDF documents

PDFWriter and Distiller can handle Type 1, TrueType or Bitmap fonts. Here is a brief description of each type:

PostScript or Type 1 Fonts

Type 1 fonts are scalable outline fonts which are defined using Post-Script's Bézier curves. Created by Adobe, oftentimes these fonts work best with RIPs because they do not need to be converted to be ripped.

TrueType Fonts

TrueType fonts are also scalable outline fonts but they are based on quadratic curves, not Bézier curves. Created by Apple and Microsoft, these fonts must either be converted to Type 1 before being ripped or a TrueType Rasterizer must be used to create the bitmap for the output device. This conversion to Type 1 or rasterizing is often invisible to the user.

Bitmap Fonts

Bitmap fonts are non-scalable pixel maps of a given typeface. To use bitmap fonts, a separate font file must be used for each size or the "jaggies" will appear on type.

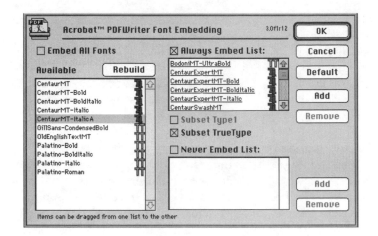

portable, font subsets can be embedded. Subsets include only the font characters used in the document which offers on average a file savings of 10K per font in the final PDF file size. If *Subset fonts* is selected and less than 35% of the characters of a font are used, PDFWriter will embed a subset of that font. If over 35% of the font characters are used, PDFWriter will automatically embed the entire font.

PDFWriter's Handling of Fonts

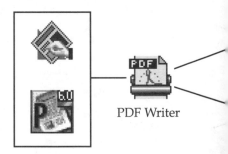

PDF Writer

PDFWriter can embed Type 1 PostScript fonts (indicated by the ▮ icon) as well as TrueType fonts (indicated by a ᵀᵀ icon). The best way to insure typographic integrity is to select *Embed All Fonts*. All fonts used in the document will be embedded in the resulting PDF file insuring correct display and printing.

Another option is to specify a list of fonts to *Always Embed* and fonts to *Never Embed*. If working in a closed Intranet system, an office where all fonts are standardized, you could place all fonts in the *Never Embed* list. This will reduce the file size by approximately 20K for each font used in the document.

Simulated Fonts
If the fonts are not embedded, PDFWriter will gather information about the font relating to its style (bold, italic), metrics (character shape) and font name. This information will be saved with the PDF file and will only require about one kilobyte of storage space. When the PDF document is used later, and the original font is available, it will be used. If the font is not available, Acrobat will use the saved font metric and style information to create an "approximate" simulation font that resembles the original, as good as possible. The *Adobe Sans Multiple Master*

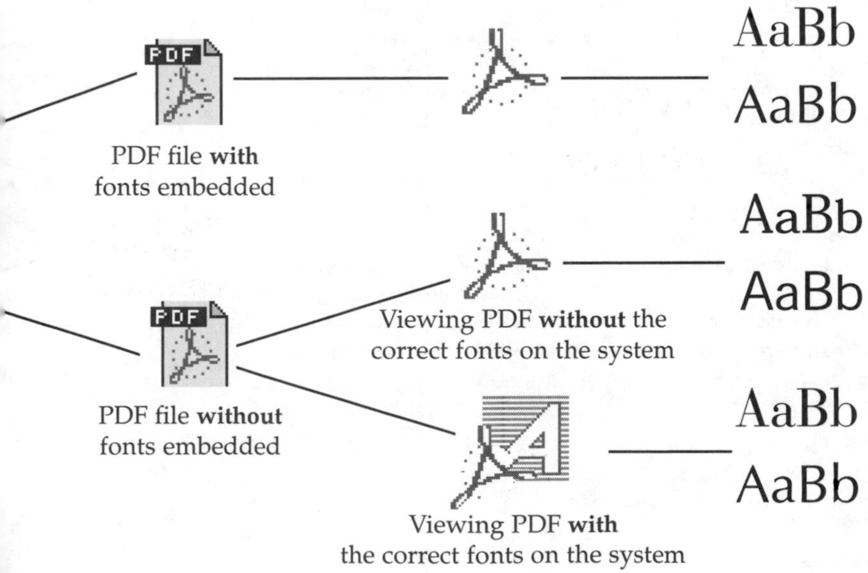

AaBb
AaBb

PDF file **with**
fonts embedded

AaBb
AaBb

Viewing PDF **without** the
correct fonts on the system

PDF file **without**
fonts embedded

AaBb
AaBb

Viewing PDF **with**
the correct fonts on the system

Helvetica light	AaBbCcDdEeFfGgHh
Gill Sans	*AaBbCcDdEeFfGgHh*
Cochin	AaBbCcDdEeFfGgHh
Garamond	*AaBbCcDdEeFfGgHh*
Bodoni	AaBbCcDdEeFfGgHh
Optima	AaBbCcDdEeFfGgHh
Stone Serif	*AaBbCcDdEeFfGgHh*
Minion	AaBbCcDdEeFfGgHh

Gill Sans

There is very little known about Nicholas Jenson especially before he in 1470 is operating as printer in Venice. The best source of information that is available about him as person is his own testament from 1480. From here it have been derived that Jenson came from southern France and that he was born at Sommevoire. It is quite certain that he had worked in the royal mint of Toryes and later Paris and that he was very successful in diemaking for coin manufacturing. King Charles VII had learned about the invention of the printing press and thought that this was a good

Minion

There is very little known about Nicholas Jenson especially before he in 1470 is operating as printer in Venice. The best source of information that is available about him as person is his own testament from 1480. From here it have been derived that Jenson came from southern France and that he was born at Sommevoire. It is quite certain that he had worked in the royal mint of Toryes and later Paris and that he was very successful in diemaking for coin manufacturing.
King Charles VII had learned about the invention of the printing press and thought that this was a good

The above illustration shows how the PDF file views/prints if the fonts were embedded in the file.

Helvetica light	AaBbCcDdEeFfGgHh
Gill Sans	AaBbCcDdEeFfGgHh
Cochin	AaBbCcDdEeFfGgHh
Garamond	AaBbCcDdEeFfGgHh
Bodoni	AaBbCcDdEeFfGgHh
Optima	AaBbCcDdEeFfGgHh
Stone Serif	AaBbCcDdEeFfGgHh
Minion	AaBbCcDdEeFfGgHh

Gill Sans

There is very little known about Nicholas Jenson especially before he in 1470 is operating as printer in Venice. The best source of information that is available about him as person is his own testament from 1480. From here it have been derived that Jenson came from southern France and that he was born at Sommevoire. It is quite certain that he had worked in the royal mint of Toryes and later Paris and that he was very successful in diemaking for coin manufacturing. King Charles VII had learned about the invention of the printing press and thought that this was a good

Minion

There is very little known about Nicholas Jenson especially before he in 1470 is operating as printer in Venice. The best source of information that is available about him as person is his own testament from 1480. From here it have been derived that Jenson came from southern France and that he was born at Sommevoire. It is quite certain that he had worked in the royal mint of Toryes and later Paris and that he was very successful in diemaking for coin manufacturing. King Charles VII had learned about the invention of the printing press and thought that this was a good

The above illustration shows how the PDF file views/prints if the fonts were simulated by Acrobat.

and the *Adobe Serif Multiple Master* are used to make these simulated fonts "on the fly."

The average reader, not including professionals in the graphic arts industry, will probably not notice that the text typeface is a simulated typeface, but as the size of the type increases, so will the chance for detection. For instance, where predominantly text-based documents contain titles or headlines of a larger type size, subsetting only the few characters that are included in the title of the document will be your best option. The subsetting of this font will insure the proper reproduction and maintain the look and feel of the document. If small file size is more important than typographic integrity, font simulation works reasonably well on most standard typefaces.

Non-standard typefaces including symbolic and ornamental typefaces are a little trickier. PDFWriter and Distiller automatically embed any fonts which they consider "non-standard." Non-standard fonts could include expert sets, swash characters or any font which does not conform to the standard glyph names described in the PostScript handbook. PDFWriter and Distiller will embed these non-standard fonts because a simulation can not be made using the Serif MM and Sans Serif MM. In the font dialog box these typefaces are underlined. If the default button is clicked, they will automatically be moved to the *Always Embed* list.

PDF Creation

The PDFWriter Print dialog box (QuarkXPress).

Once options for font embedding and compression have been chosen, creating a PDF is as simple as hitting the *Print* button.

1. Select *Print* from the *File* Menu
2. Name the resulting PDF file
3. Determine where the file is to be saved
4. PDFWriter handles the rest

PDFWriter Overview

Even though PDFWriter is extremely convenient and is the easiest way to prepare PDF files, it is not without drawbacks. First, applications do not "see" the PDFWriter as a PostScript printer, which means Encapsulated PostScript (EPS) images will be sent to PDFWriter as low-resolution rough screen versions. Also, PDFWriter cannot be used with Apple's page display and description format, *QuickDraw GX*. If QuickDraw GX is installed, PDFWriter will not be displayed in the Chooser.

As a general rule, if your document contains EPS images or you would like more control over the compression and font embedding options, Acrobat Distiller should be used to create the PDF.

PDFWriter does not support all controls that are supported in a PDF file. And as mentioned above, PDFWriter is a non PostScript printer driver, and the information will not be treated the same way as if the file was printed to a PostScript printer. To solve this problem, Acrobat Distiller must be used.

PDFWriter is good for "fast" PDF creation. It is almost as simple as printing a document to a printer. However, it does not allow the control and quality available using Distiller.

Acrobat Distiller

What Distiller lacks in ease of use is more than made up in its reliability and extended capabilities over PDFWriter. Distiller can be seen as a software RIP, where the PostScript codes are interpreted and an object list is generated. But instead of generating a raster representation of the page, it is formatted into a PDF document. In version 3.0 of Distiller, version 1.2 of PDF is used. The major difference from the previous PDF versions, 1.0 and 1.1 is that PostScript commands for professional print production are included. Some of these features are accessed in Acrobat Distiller, and for other functions, third party plug-ins must be developed to take full advantage of the possibilities of PDF 1.2.

Why use Distiller vs. PDFWriter?
1. *For more control over compression and font embedding options.*
2. *Your document contains EPS images.*
3. *To distill PostScript files from another platform*
4. *You encounter problems using PDFWriter*

Distiller can create PDF documents from both EPS and PostScript files.

Creating a PDF with Distiller requires first "saving" the document to a PostScript file (the data that would have been sent to a printer is instead saved in a file) and then opening that file in Distiller. The advantage of creating a PDF this way is that all of the data necessary to render the page is described in the PostScript file. As a result, Distiller can also act as a preflight tool to ensure that jobs are "RIP-able." Chances are that if it distills, it will print. Another advantage of Distiller is that it offers more control over compression and font options than PDF-Writer. High-end printing controls are also available through Distiller.

Creating PDF with Distiller

The first step in creating PDF documents with Distiller is to produce a PostScript file. Because the PostScript file is going to be used to generate the PDF document, the correct page setup options must be set here. If the page orientation is not correct at this point, it cannot be corrected in Distiller.

When using QuarkXPress, it is also important to use the Acrobat Distiller printer description in the Page Setup menu. If a black and white printer description (most laser printers) is selected, the resulting PDF will be in black and white. This is also helpful if you choose to use a Custom Page size not supported by the selected printer description.

After the correct Page Setup options have been chosen, select Print under the File menu.

1. Choose the radio button *File* in the *Destination* box.
2. With this selected, the *Print* button will change to *Save*.

When making a PDF with Distiller you must have a PostScript file first. This is created by choosing a PostScript printer driver in the Chooser and when in the print dialog box making sure that File is chosen as destination. Notice that the "Print" button changes to "Save".

If you are creating a PDF file with colors, it is crucial to choose a color PPD (like the Acrobat Distiller PPD) when creating the PostScript. If this is not done, the result will be a black and white PDF document.

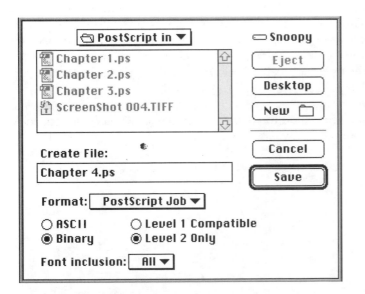

Printer: "Gutenberg"   8.3.3   **Save**

Copies: 1   Pages: ⦿ All   ○ From: ☐   To: ☐   **Cancel**

Paper Source
⦿ All ○ First from: Cassette ▼   **Destination**   **Options**
Remaining from: Cassette ▼   ○ Printer   **Help**
   ⦿ File

Page Sequence: All   ☐ Collate   ☐ Back to Front
Output: Normal   ☐ Spreads   ☐ Thumbnails
Tiling: Off   Overlap: 3"
Separation: Off   Plate: All Plates
Registration: Off   OPI: Include Images
Options: ☐ Calibrated Output   ☐ Print Colors as Grays
      ☐ Include Blank Pages

3. Click on Save
4. Name the PostScript file and designate the location where it will be saved

📁 PostScript in ▼   💾 Snoopy

🖹 Chapter 1.ps   **Eject**
🖹 Chapter 2.ps
🖹 Chapter 3.ps   **Desktop**
🖹 ScreenShot 004.TIFF
         New 📁

Create File: **Cancel**
Chapter 4.ps   **Save**

Format: PostScript Job ▼

○ ASCII   ○ Level 1 Compatible
⦿ Binary   ⦿ Level 2 Only

Font inclusion: All ▼

5. Select either PostScript Level 1 or Level 2. Since Distiller is a Level 2 RIP, it's best to select Level 2. If you have problems distilling the file, try using Level 1.

To insure that Distiller has all of the font information necessary to properly produce the PDF document, be sure to select include "All", "All but Standard 13" under the font inclusion menu when saving the PostScript file. Although this will add to the overall size of the PostScript file, PostScript is only an intermediary step to the PDF creation. It can be discarded once the PDF document has been created.

Including Fonts vs. Embedding Fonts

Including fonts in a PostScript file is not the same thing as embedding them in a PDF document. Including them with the PostScript file ensures that Distiller will have access to them when it creates the PDF. Only Distiller and PDFWriter can embed fonts in PDF documents.

6. Determine the font inclusion—None, All, All but the standard thirteen, All but those in the PPD file.

All: All typefaces that are used in the file will be embedded in the PostScript file.

All but Standard 13: There are thirteen fonts that always are included in a PostScript printer (Courier, Courier bold, Courier italic, Courier bold italic, Helvetica, Helvetica bold, Helvetica italic, Helvetica bold italic, Times, Times bold, Times italic, Times bold italic).

All but Fonts in PPD File: This will send all fonts not included in the PostScript Printer Description (PPD). The PPD file contains information about the fonts installed on the output device. If the Distiller PPD is being used, there should be no problem. But if you are using a PPD for a printer with installed fonts not available to Distiller, you could get Courier in your PDF file.

The best advice is to include *All* fonts in the PostScript file. It is possible to not include the fonts and then make sure that Distiller knows where to find them for PDF creation. However, the foolproof method is to include them in the PostScript.

After all options for the PostScript file have been chosen, click on the Save button and the PostScript file will be generated.

Distilling PostScript Files

Creating PDF files from PostScript is as simple as opening Distiller, selecting *Open* from the *File* menu and naming the resulting PDF document. Although the actual process is easy, setting up how the PostScript file will be distilled into a PDF document requires a little preparation.

```
═══════════ Acrobat Distiller ═══════════

       Status: Distilling "Document2.ps"
         Size: 381K Bytes
       Source: User Selection

   Percent Read: 22%          Page:
   ████████▒▒▒▒▒▒▒▒▒▒▒▒▒▒▒▒▒▒▒▒▒▒▒▒▒▒▒

      [ Cancel Job ]  [ Pause ]

   Messages
   Distilling: Document2.ps
   Source: Snoopy :Desktop Folder :All PDF Book Files :Chapter 5 :Document2.ps
   Destination: Snoopy :Desktop Folder :All PDF Book Files :Chapter 5 :Document2.pdf
   Start Time: Tuesday, January 28, 1997 at 4:47 PM
```

Understating the power of the software engine underneath, the Distiller opening window is deceivingly simple. The Cancel Job button can be used to flush a job in the middle of processing. The Pause button prevents Distiller from accepting any new jobs until the Resume button is pushed (just like taking a RIP offline). If the Pause button is pushed in the middle of processing a job, it will finish the job and then Pause. It cannot pause in the middle of a job

Distiller Job Options

This is the heart of customizing PDF documents within Distiller and is available in the Distiller menu. There are four sections to *Job Options*:

1. *General*
2. *Compression*
3. *Font embedding*
4. *Advanced*

General

Most of the General settings resemble those available within PDFWriter. However, there are added controls for Default resolution and Default page size. If the page size is not specified within the PostScript file, the page size will be set by the value placed here. This is useful for distilling EPS files which do not contain any page size information. If the page size is specified within the PostScript file, Distiller will use the specified size not Distiller's default.

Distiller General Options

General ⟍Compression ⟍Font Embedding ⟍Advanced⟍

File Settings
Compatibility: [Acrobat 3.0]
☐ ASCII Format

Device Settings
Default Resolution: [300] dpi
Default Page Size:
Width: [8.50] x Height: [11.00] [Inches]

[OK]
[Cancel]
[Defaults]

Compression

Distiller offers more control over compression options than PDFWriter. The *Automatic Compression* option in Distiller evaluates images in a file and applies the "best" compression scheme. If the image consists of many gradual tone changes, as in a photograph, JPEG is used, but if sharp edges are present, such as in screen dumps and line art graphics, LZW/ZIP (depending on the Compatibility setting chosen in General options) is used. The user can specify which level of JPEG compression should be used.

In the Compression part of Job options, the user can choose between the different image compression schemes that are available. All compression can also be turned off.

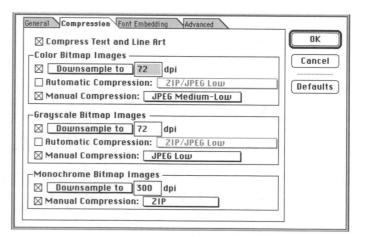

General ⟍**Compression** ⟍Font Embedding ⟍Advanced⟍

☒ Compress Text and Line Art
Color Bitmap Images
☒ [Downsample to] [72] dpi
☐ Automatic Compression: [ZIP/JPEG Low]
☒ Manual Compression: [JPEG Medium-Low]

Grayscale Bitmap Images
☒ [Downsample to] [72] dpi
☐ Automatic Compression: [ZIP/JPEG Low]
☒ Manual Compression: [JPEG Low]

Monochrome Bitmap Images
☒ [Downsample to] [300] dpi
☒ Manual Compression: [ZIP]

[OK]
[Cancel]
[Defaults]

If individual control over the compression is desired, click *Automatic Compression* off and select *Manual Compression*. This lets the user specify exactly which type of compression should be used for color, grayscale and monochrome bitmap images.

Also new to Distiller, and not available in PDFWriter, is the *Subsample to* option. Both downsampling and subsampling reduce the resolution of images and overall file size, however, they use different approaches. Downsampling evaluates the pixels in an array, averages those values into a larger remaining pixel that covers the same area. Subsampling selects the value of the center pixel in an array, discards the remaining pixels and creates a pixel with the center value covering the same area as the array. Basically, downsampling averages pixel data and subsampling selects the center pixel and discards the other pixel data. Both subsampling and downsampling can be set to specific resolutions as low as 9 dpi.

Downsampling can be used efficiently for production printing. For example, a PostScript stream made from a 400 dpi file for an advertisement can be distilled into a PDF downsampled to 350 dpi for use with a 175 lpi screen in a magazine. That same stream can be distilled into a PDF downsampled to 170 dpi so it can be repurposed to print in a newspaper where the screen ruling is 80 lpi. This repurposing using downsampling can be done without alteration to the original file or original scans.

Font Embedding

Again, font embedding controls are similar to PDFWriter but with finer control over when fonts are subsetted. By decreasing the threshold, more entire fonts will be embedded, thus increasing the overall file size of the PDF. Distiller allows the subsetting threshold to be set by the user. Instead of PDFWriter's default of 35%, the user can specify any value from 1 to 99%. Just as in PDFWriter, if the threshold is exceeded, the entire font will be embedded.

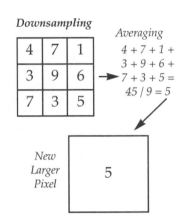

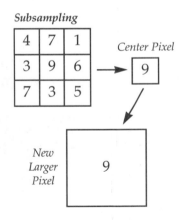

Downsampling

Downsampled to 150 dpi.
Distilling time: 13 seconds.

Downsampled to 72 dpi.
Distilling time: 13 seconds.

Full resolution 300 dpi
Distilling time: 22 seconds.

Downsampling averages tone values from surrounding pixels, and reproduces the average tone using one larger pixel. This is a method that takes more computing power and is slower than subsampling, although the quality is better.

Because downsampling averages pixels, the picture becomes more fuzzy, but look better compared to subsampling especially with big reductions in resolution.

If Downsample Images is selected in PDFWriter, it will automatically downsample images to 72 dpi or the closest possible value. Distiller allows you to specify the downsample resolution.

Subsampling

Subsampled to 150 dpi.
Distilling time: 12 seconds.

Subsampled to 72 dpi.
Distilling time: 10 seconds.

Full resolution 300 dpi
Distilling time: 22 seconds.

Subsampling takes the center pixel's value and applies it to the larger resulting pixel. This does not produce as accurate a reproduction as downsampling. Subsampling produces a less fuzzy image compared to downsampling, but on the other hand the pixels are very noticeable when subsampling from high resolution to very low resolutions. The picture begins to look "blocky."

Subsampling can only be accomplished using Distiller. Because subsampling requires less computing power, Subsampling takes less time to distill than does downsampling.

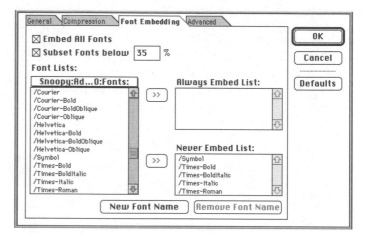

Distiller Font Embedding Options

Another difference between PDFWriter and Distiller is font availability. Since PDFWriter creates PDF documents directly from the layout application, all fonts used in the document are available for embedding or substitution information. Because Distiller can be run either on the local computer that generated the PostScript file or on a Network Server, the fonts may not be available. If Distiller cannot reference the fonts, there is a risk that fonts will be missing and possibly not even simulated. To be certain that this does not happen, two methods are possible. The easiest way is to include the fonts in the PostScript file prior to distilling. The second method is to tell Distiller where the fonts can be found. To do this, select *Font Locations* under the *Distiller* menu. Although there is always a risk that the font used in the file may not be available in the font location and then `Courier` will be used.

To insure that proper fonts have been embedded you can open the PDF document in Reader or Exchange on a computer which does not have the fonts. Select File—Document Info—Fonts. Under the "Used Font" category, the listings should read "Embedded" or "Embedded Subset."

The *Font Embedding* section of *Job Options* lists available fonts. If the *Embed All Fonts* box is checked, all fonts used in the document will be embedded. If a font is not to be embedded, Distiller will retrieve the font metrics so that a simulation using the Serif MM or Sans Serif MM can be made.

When creating PDF files, Distiller looks for fonts or font metric information in the following manner:
- In the PostScript file
- In the *Font Locations* menu (which by default includes sys-

tem folder locations as well as Acrobat's font folder). Distiller also looks in locations specified by a font management utility like *Suitcase*.

- The font database that is installed with Acrobat. This database contains the information necessary to produce simulation fonts for Adobe's Type 1 font library. However, since new fonts are released everyday, and not all by Adobe, you have yet another reason to include the fonts in the PostScript file.

If after searching all of these locations, Distiller still cannot find the required font information, our old friend `Courier` will be used as a substitute font.

Advanced Options

With the release of Acrobat 3.0, Adobe has addressed some of the needs of the high-end printing market. Probably the most important for printing applications is the ability to include overprint settings and preserve halftone screen information.

Prologue and Epilogue Comments

The check box *Distill with prologue.ps/epilogue.ps* is important when you want to retain spot colors (defined as separation color spaces in PostScript) when creating a PDF file. If you do not use these epilogue/prologue files then spot colors will get mapped to process colors during the conversion to PDF

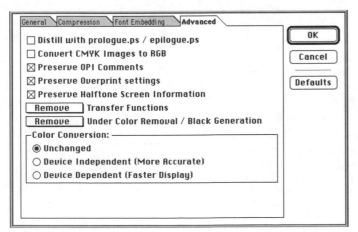

Distiller's Advanced Options

Distiller's
Handling of Fonts

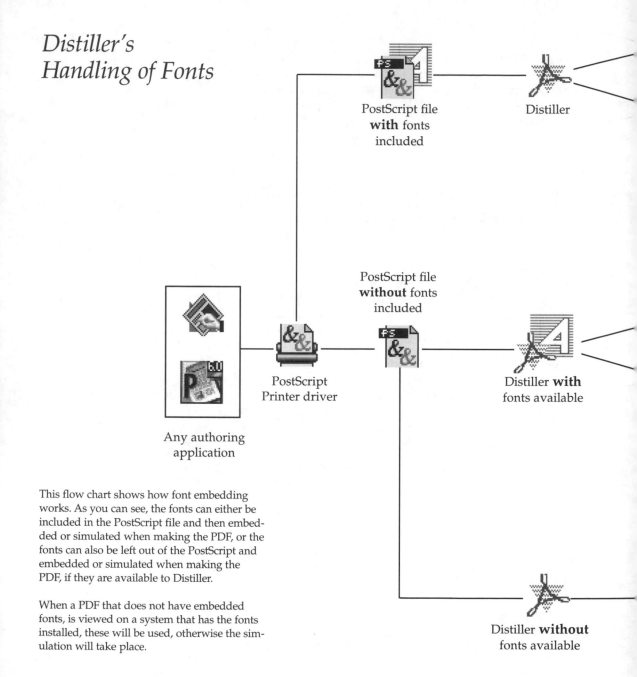

PostScript file
with fonts
included

Distiller

PostScript file
without fonts
included

Any authoring
application

PostScript
Printer driver

Distiller **with**
fonts available

This flow chart shows how font embedding
works. As you can see, the fonts can either be
included in the PostScript file and then embedded or simulated when making the PDF, or the
fonts can also be left out of the PostScript and
embedded or simulated when making the
PDF, if they are available to Distiller.

When a PDF that does not have embedded
fonts, is viewed on a system that has the fonts
installed, these will be used, otherwise the simulation will take place.

Distiller **without**
fonts available

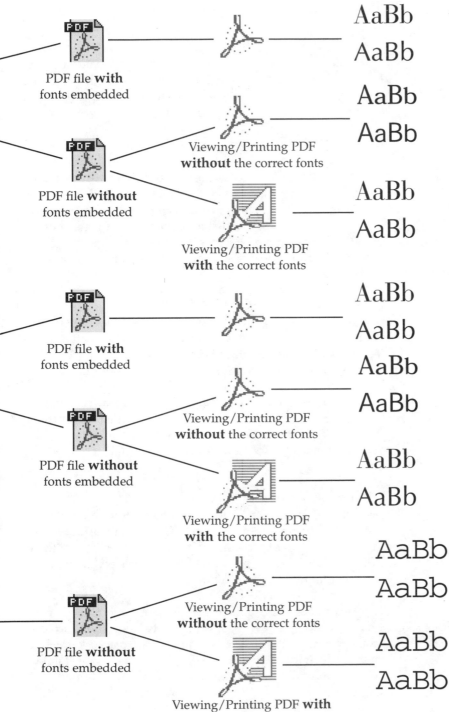

PDF file **with**
fonts embedded

Viewing/Printing PDF
without the correct fonts

Viewing/Printing PDF
with the correct fonts

PDF file **without**
fonts embedded

PDF file **with**
fonts embedded

Viewing/Printing PDF
without the correct fonts

Viewing/Printing PDF
with the correct fonts

PDF file **without**
fonts embedded

Viewing/Printing PDF
without the correct fonts

Viewing/Printing PDF **with**
the correct fonts

PDF file **without**
fonts embedded

The default prologue.ps and epilogue.ps file included in the High-End folder of Acrobat will preserve spot colors as they are defined. To be used the prologue.ps and epilogue.ps files must be located in the same root folder as the Distiller application.

In a way, the functionality of the prologue/epilogue is similar to a PPD file. PPDs can contain snippets of PostScript that get included in a PostScript file. In the case of PPDs, a driver parses the PPD and determines where in the PostScript file being created to insert that PostScript code. The prologue/epilogue are PostScript files themselves that are specific to the context of the Distiller. The functionality would be the same as inserting additional PostScript code at the front or back of a PostScript file to be distilled.

Convert CMYK Images to RGB
Also offered is the option of converting CMYK files to RGB during PDF creation. RGB files are smaller than CMYK files making the PDF file more compact. This is also helpful for Web distribution since monitors display RGB and not CMYK.

However, if the goal is to send the PDF file to a digital press or high-end output device, leave this box unchecked. Color transforms back and forth between CMYK and RGB degrade color quality in images. To convert images to RGB, click on the *Convert CMYK Images to RGB*.

Preserve OPI Comments
Distiller can also preserve Open Pre-press Interface (OPI) comments allowing for low-resolution FPO images to be placed into a PDF reducing overall file size. The PDF can then be sent to the OPI server and the low resolution FPO images will be replaced with their high-resolution counterparts.

The idea is that large image files do not have to be moved around on storage devices or on the network. When the composite page is produced, the FPO images are placed in the document. When printed to the OPI server, the low-resolution information will be exchanged for the high-resolution images. To preserve OPI comments when Distilling, make sure that the *Preserve OPI Comments* box is checked.

Preserve Overprint Settings

Another new function in 3.0 is that overprint and choke/spread information can be preserved. Often called trapping, choking/spreading is used to make press misregister less apparent when two colors butt against one another. Overprints can also be used for black type on a colored background. With this box checked, Distiller will retain the overprint, otherwise the underlying layer will be "knocked out."

Preserve Halftone Screen Information

Screening information can be preserved from the initial PostScript file so when output from Exchange, the screening information is retained. Now images with various screen angles, line screen rulings, and dot shapes can be output at the desired settings, not the imagesetter's default setting. To preserve preselected screens, make sure that the *Preserve Halftone Screen Information* box is checked.

Transfer Functions

PostScript comments regarding transfer functions can also be handled by Distiller. If *Preserve* is selected, any transfer curves will be saved along with the PDF document. The curves can later be applied to the image when the PDF is printed to a RIP that supports transfer functions. This is the equivalent of what Photoshop does when it saves transfer functions—it saves the curve but does not change the actual data of the image file.

If *Apply* is selected, the actual data of the image file will be changed when saved in the PDF document. This means that the image on screen, as well as when printed, will be changed. Selecting *Remove* will delete the transfer function from the PDF document. Since transfer curves are designed to adjust image reproduction on a specific output device, PDF documents for general distribution should remove any transfer curves.

Under Color Removal/Black Generation

Distiller 3.0 also allows for *Under Color Removal/Black Generation* to be preserved or removed in a PDF document. This information is used in the RGB to CMYK conversion process and is generally output device-specific. If the PDF document is intended for general distribution, this information should be removed.

Although Distiller can preserve trapping settings, some page layout programs do not send trapping information with composite PostScript files. For instance, QuarkXPress traps are only sent in the PostScript file when output to separations. The end result is no trapping. If traps are set within illustration programs like Illustrator or Freehand, Distiller will preserve the trap information.

Transfer functions are used to adjust the reproduction of an image on a specific output device. Acrobat 3.0 allows transfer functions, sometimes called transfer curves, to be applied, preserved or removed.

Color Conversions

Distiller also allows users to specify how color images in the file are defined in terms of color space and device-dependency. The default *Unchanged* option leaves color images in the color space in which they are defined.

With the *Device Independent* option selected, color objects not already mapped to calibrated spaces are converted to device-independent spaces like LAB. Device-dependent CMYK images are also converted into LAB space while device-dependent RGB files are converted to a Calibrated RGB space.

Selecting the *Device Dependent* option in Distiller will convert device independent images to device dependent RGB space. If on-screen display speed is an issue, as it is in Web-publishing, this is the best option to choose.

The Remaining Half of Creating PDF

With PS Printer 8.3.1. it is possible to make a PDF file directly from the print dialog box, even though Distiller will still be used for the conversion from PostScript to PDF.

It was mentioned in the beginning of the chapter that there are actually two and a half ways to create PDF files. The other half is to use Distiller Assistant and the Adobe PSPrinter Printer Driver.

The wonder of it is really scripting. Using the *Virtual Printer* option of PSPrinter, *PDF* shows up as a third way to send PostScript files in the *Print* dialog box of most applications. When this button is selected, the PostScript is saved, Distiller is opened and the PostScript file is distilled. After the PDF file is created the PostScript file is optionally discarded.

Now it is primarily an automation tool for a user, the potential for extended capabilities is evident. For example in Adobe

PageMaker 6.0, the user can decide if the table of contents should be made into a bookmark file, index words can be made into links, the text flow can be defined as an article so that reading on screen is easier. (For definitions on bookmarks, links, and articles, continue on to the next chapter).

A disadvantage is that you have to set up Distiller options in advance as PS Printer 8.3.1 does not offer the font embedding and compression options.

Distilling on a Network

In a production setting, Distiller can be set up on a dedicated network computer where a number of users can drop PostScript files into a *Watched Folder*. When Distiller encounters a PostScript file in this folder, it will create the PDF and place the file into an "out" folder where network users can then move or use the files.

The Watched folder dialog box defines what settings Distiller will be using when PostScript files are put into the different hot folders.

Each of these Watched folders, can be set to provide different compression and font embedding options. One folder could be designated for interoffice distribution with no font embedding. Another folder could be set for distilling PDFs for Web distrib-

By using hot folders the PDF production can be made easier when making PDF files for different usages.

ution by downsampling the images. This allows for the multi-purpose workflow.

To set up a folders, select the *Watched Folders* selection under the Distiller menu. Options can be set for when and where Distiller looks for PostScript files as well as what is done with the original PostScript file.

End Comments
Acrobat 3.0 and the PDF format offer great versatility for Web-based publishing and high-end publishing applications. Choosing the right options reverts back to an end-use analysis.

Using Distiller on a network for the Multi-Purpose Workflow

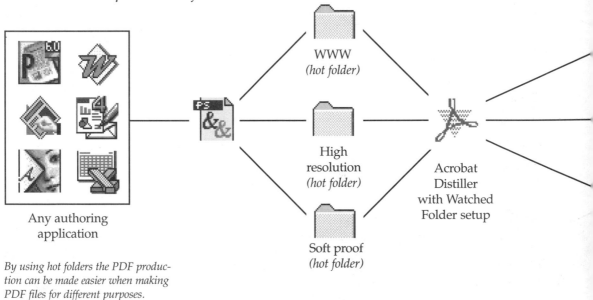

Any authoring
application

WWW
(hot folder)

High
resolution
(hot folder)

Soft proof
(hot folder)

Acrobat
Distiller
with Watched
Folder setup

By using hot folders the PDF production can be made easier when making PDF files for different purposes.

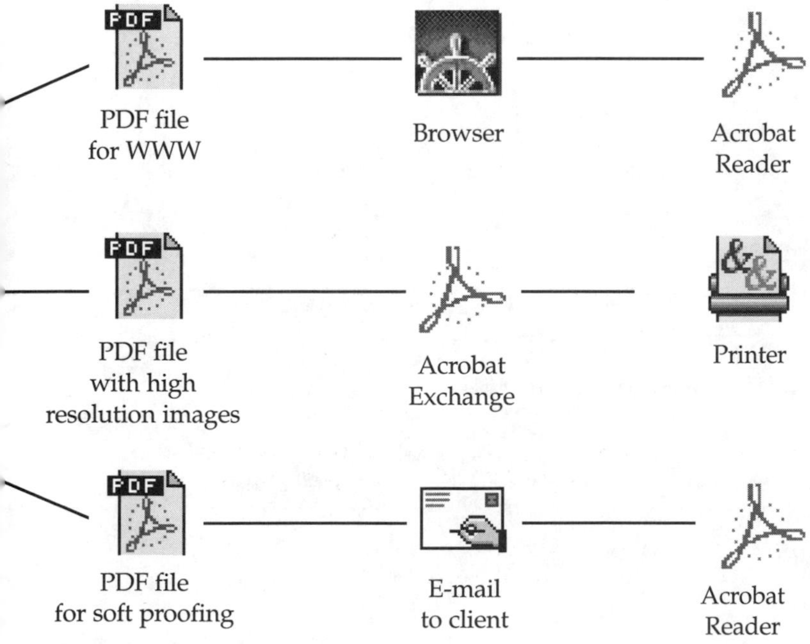

PDF file
for WWW

Browser

Acrobat
Reader

PDF file
with high
resolution images

Acrobat
Exchange

Printer

PDF file
for soft proofing

E-mail
to client

Acrobat
Reader

Sample Settings for High-End Print PDF

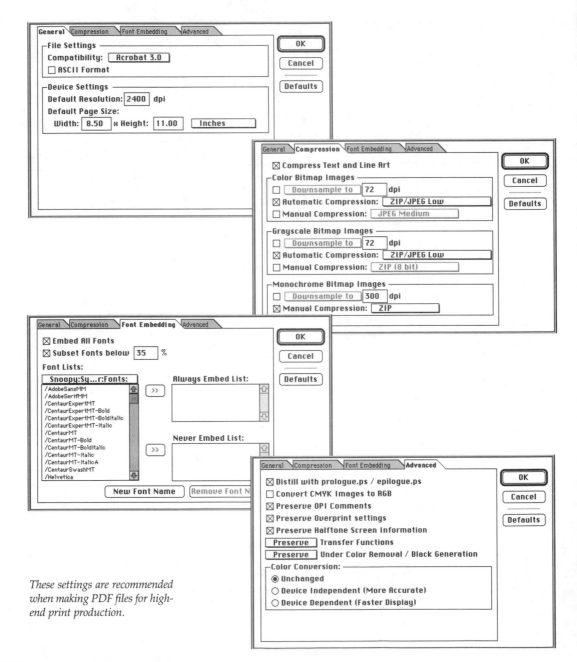

These settings are recommended when making PDF files for high-end print production.

Sample Settings for Web-Based PDF Distribution

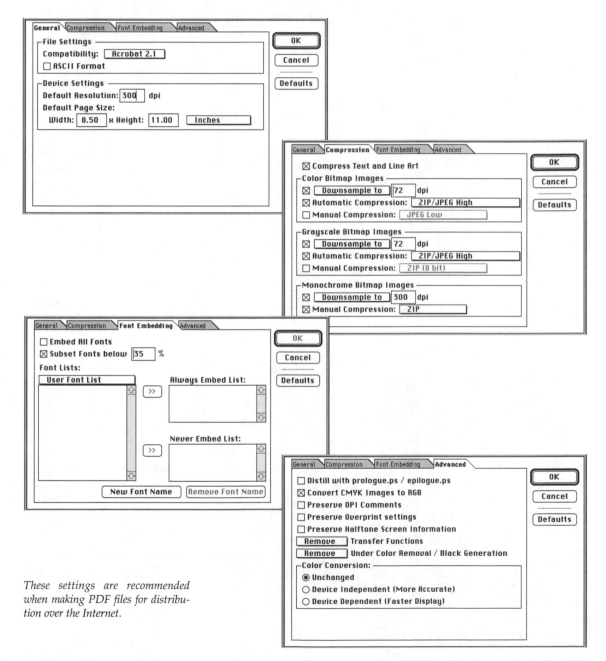

These settings are recommended when making PDF files for distribution over the Internet.

CHAPTER

USING PDF FILES

Exchange and Reader are the two applications of the Acrobat suite which allow the user to view, navigate, search, print, modify, and enhance the PDF documents created in Distiller or PDFWriter. They are key parts of using and applying PDFs.

While the ideal digital document would be wholly application-independent, the PDF format is reliant upon either Exchange or Reader to be viewed or printed. Reader, the simplest way to access PDF files, allows for the viewing, navigating, searching, and printing of PDF documents. Exchange goes one step further by including many editing features. Some new features available in Acrobat version 3.0 include enhanced security options, customizable forms, and page-on-demand Web access.

Exchange
Exchange is the essence of accessing and working with PDF documents. Distiller creates PDF documents and Exchange customizes them. Exchange includes tools for enhancing PDF documents which build interactivity and security options into PDF documents, while allowing certain levels of editability such as the ordering of pages and text touch-ups.

Working with Exchange can be broken down into four logical areas: Viewing/Navigating, Editing, Interactivity Options and Security Options.

Viewing PDF Documents

Becoming acquainted with Exchange is like a child taking its first steps or reading its first sentence. Learning incrementally adds up to understanding the whole. Learning how to effectively view and move through a PDF document is like that taking that first step to understanding the whole application.

Page View Options

Exchange allows for the screen viewing of the page to be handled in many different fashions. Many of the viewing capabilities are similar to those of page layout programs and general platform software.

In addition to the display of the actual page contents, PDF documents can also carry information regarding the logical layout of the document. Enhancements such as bookmarks and thumbnails for the pages can be saved within the PDF document making navigating through the PDF a simple process.

Page Only, Bookmarks, Thumbnail Views

Page only

Bookmarks

Thumbnails

The tool bar offers some direct layout functions. The *Page Only* view does just what it says, it shows just the page on the screen. The *Bookmark* view splits the screen and brings up any previously created bookmarks in the left portion of the screen. The *Bookmark* view must be activated when creating new bookmarks as well. The *Thumbnail* view also splits the screen and shows any already created thumbnails in the left portion of the screen. By the way, 21" monitors are almost mandatory.

Single, Continuous, and Continuous Facing Pages

Exchange enables the user to designate the document view when scrolling through the pages. *Single page, Continuous page,* and *Continuous Facing pages* are options under the view window.

Single Page View displays only the current page in the window, while *Continuous Page View* will display documents in a scrolling fashion, allowing for the bottom of one page and the top of the next to be split on the screen. The *Continuous Facing Page* option displays pages in a spread type fashion which is useful for pages designed for magazine spread publication. A centerfold image would lose its pizazz if the two pages that make up the spread had to be viewed separately.

Continuous facing pages will not change the layout in the thumbnail view.

Actual Size, Fit Page, and Fit Width

Page view options control how the document is going to be displayed in the monitor—*Actual size, Fit page, and Fit width. Actual Size* is a 100% view of the document, *Fit page* fits the entire document into the window, and *Fit width*, well, fits the width of the document in the window.

Magnifying Glass

The magnifying glass found on the tool bar and accessed from the main menu bar, allows for magnification at a number of predetermined percentages. The pop-up window accessed by the magnifying glass on the bottom page bar offers these predetermined percentages as well as a a user-defined percentage. This window also allows for *Fit Page, Fit Width, and Fit Visible* view options. Similar to most applications, the magnifying glass will become a reduction glass when the option key is held down.

Create Thumbnails

Thumbnails are small display versions of the pages within a PDF document. The creation of thumbnails is a great viewing capability when the goal is page insertion/deletion, or editing the page layout. Thumbnails are also very useful when viewing the contents of the pages. By scrolling through the thumbnails and clicking on the page you wish to view, that page appears in the page view portion of the screen.

By simply dragging down the Document window on the main menu bar and selecting *Create All Thumbnails*, the small page versions are automatically created and displayed. When thumbnails are created, a window opens to the left of the page view window, splitting the screen into two frames.

When initially creating thumbnails, they appear automatically, but they can be hidden by clicking on the *Page Only* icon on the

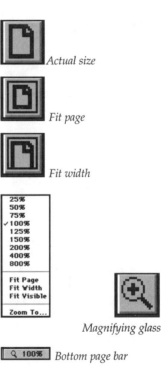

Actual size

Fit page

Fit width

25%
50%
75%
✓100%
125%
150%
200%
400%
800%

Fit Page
Fit Width
Fit Visible

Zoom To...

Magnifying glass

🔍 100% *Bottom page bar*

Create Thumbnails

Thumbnail View

Exchange automatically numbers the thumbnail pages beginning with one and continuing consecutively in number order. The numbering is not related to any previous numbering in the document itself.

If you select the Thumbnails view option and thumbnails have not been previously created, blank thumbnails will appear.

First   Next
Page   Page

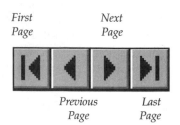

Previous   Last
Page   Page

tool bar or by selecting *Page only* from the view window in the main menu bar. If you want to call up thumbnails you know have been created, or you want to check and see if they have been created, simply select the *Thumbnails* icon in the tool bar.

Thumbnails are the most efficient way to move, copy, and delete pages within a single document, or insert pages from another document. These capabilities are editing issues and will be further discussed in the Editing section of this chapter. Once the thumbnail view is selected, thumbnails can be scrolled and clicked on to view the respective page.

Thumbnails are an all-or-nothing entity in Acrobat—either every page has a thumbnail or none of them do. The creation of thumbnails will increase the file size of the PDF document about 30%. So, if size is a crucial consideration, you might choose to skip thumbnails.

Navigating Through PDF Documents
As already discussed, one efficient way of navigating through pages is the use of thumbnails. The tool bar also offers for simple page navigation tools. *First page, Previous page, Next page,* and *Last page* are all accessible with a simple click on the respec-

tive tool icon. Again, these destinations can be reached from the view window under the main menu bar or through shortcut commands.

Go Forward and Go Backward are other navigation tools found on the tool bar. For instance, selecting Go Backward will bring you back to your previous page and viewing situation. For instance, if you had jumped from page 3 to page 64, *Go Backward* would return you to page 3 at the magnification you had been viewing the page. These commands can also be completed under the View window and shortcut commands. Exchange remembers 64 movements for this function.

Bookmarks

Bookmarks are another navigation tool, serving a purpose similar to that of an index or outline. The user can become oriented with the document page layout quickly and can easily navigate through an extensive file quite quickly. Bookmarks are strictly word-based as opposed to the thumbnail's image-based capabilities. Bookmarks, however, account for less file size.

Once the *Bookmarks view* has been selected, the creation is rather simple:
1. Position the page on the screen exactly as the viewer should see it.
2. Select *New bookmark* from the document window on the main menu bar. (A page icon appears with the temporary name "Untitled.")
3. Type the name for the bookmark.

Bookmarks may be positioned as a sub-bookmark to create a true outline hierarchical structure. Once the bookmark is created (or when it is still untitled) it can be dragged down to the right to a sub-position and can also be dragged out of a sub-position by dragging it to the left again. Basically, once marks are created, they can be repositioned to any location in the hierarchical structure. Bookmarks may be edited by:
1. Again, position the page on the screen exactly as the viewer should see it.
2. Click on the page icon to highlight the bookmark intended to be changed.

Go Forward

Go Back

Do not confuse Go Backward and Go Forward with Undo and Redo. These commands remember viewing conditions, not editing selections.

If the goal is to keep the PDF file size small, thumbnails can easily be deleted by selecting Delete All Thumbnails under the Document window on the main menu bar. Just remember that if thumbnails are not created or are deleted in Exchange, they cannot be viewed in Reader.

Document
Set Page Action...
Crop Pages...
Rotate Pages...   ⌘⇧O

Insert Pages...   ⌘⇧I
Extract Pages...   ⌘⇧E
Replace Pages...   ⌘⇧R
Delete Pages...   ⌘⇧D

New Bookmark   ⌘B
Reset Bookmark Destination ⌃⌘R

Create All Thumbnails
Delete All Thumbnails

Create Bookmarks

Bookmarks view

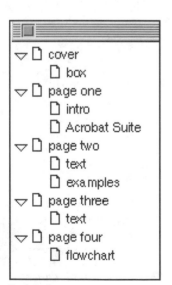

Bookmarks

3. Select *Reset Bookmark Destination* from the Document window on the main menu bar.
4. Click on *Yes* when asked if you really want to do this.

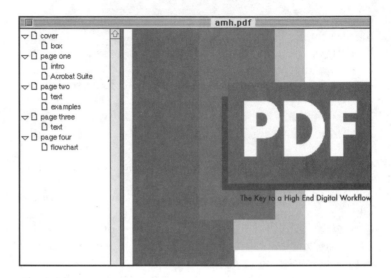

Bookmarks may be deleted by selecting the bookmark and pressing the Delete key.

Creating Articles

One of the worst aspects of on-screen digital publications is that they are not nearly as easy to read as the hardcopy publication. Trying to read a digital article requires enlarging to a readable level and then reducing it so navigating to the next article thread is possible. Acrobat Articles are a navigation tool that can be built into PDF documents to allow easy reading of selected text, or an entire article, throughout the PDF.

Acrobat's *Article* function solves much of the difficulty by enlarging the text to a readable level and following the article through the document. Much like a jump line in a newspaper article directs the reader where the article continues, the Article tool leads the PDF user throughout a document following the pre-defined path of text.

The *Article* tool of Acrobat is similar to a hypertext link (the text you click on in a Web page that jumps you to a different location). However, information regarding the article title, subject, author and keywords can also be included. A list of articles for a PDF document can be viewed.

To set up an article within a PDF document, select the *Article* tool under the *Tools* menu. The screen pointer becomes a set of crosshairs that are used to marquee text. Each successive area of text in the article is marqueed until the article is completely defined.

As users click on articles in a PDF, the pre-defined sections are enlarged to a readable level. As readers approach the bottom of the screen and click again, more of the article is displayed allowing for easier reading of on-screen text. Print applications for this feature are virtually none, but Articles provide an excellent tool for electronic publications.

Interactivity Options
PDF documents can have options like hypertext links, Quick-Time movies and forms added making them more interactive.

Creating Links
Links are useful tools that build interactivity between the user and the document by performing actions when clicked. Activated links can perform a number of operations including jumping to a referred Web site, jumping to another section of the PDF document, or playing a QuickTime movie.

Any portion of a PDF document can have a link associated with it. When the link tool is selected, users marquee the area that will be sensitive to the link—as small as a word or line or as large as the page.

After the selection has been marqueed, the link attributes window is displayed. The top half of the dialog box deals with the appearance of the link—visible or invisible. If the link is selected to be visible, the characteristics of the link bounding box can be defined. For instance, the border of the link box can be set to either thin, medium or thick settings, the color can be changed, and the effect when the link is clicked can be selected.

Tools	
🖐 Hand	⌘⌥1
🔍 Zoom In	⌘⌥2
🔍 Zoom Out	⌘⌥3
Select Text	⌘⌥4
Select Graphics	⌘⌥5
📄 Note	⌘⌥6
🔗 Link	⌘⌥7
✓ Article	⌘⌥8
Form	
Movie	
T TouchUp Text	
Find...	⌘F
Find Again	⌘G
Find Next Note	⌘T
Summarize Notes	⌘⇧T
Search	▶

Creating Articles

Link tool

The Link tool allows Exchange users to specify actions for user-selected areas of the PDF document.

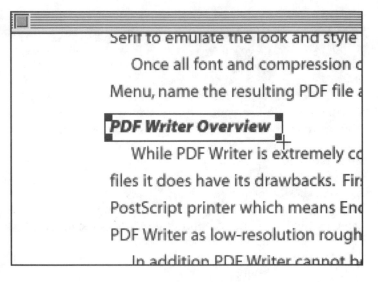

Setting Links within Exchange

Care should be taken not to create links that can't be followed. For instance, an Execute Menu item command referring to a Menu Item available in Exchange, but not in Reader, will add to user confusion and unnecessarily clutter the file.

Movie data will not be saved with the PDF file. Only a reference to its location on the hard drive or network is saved in the file. The movie file must also be distributed ultimately reducing the portability of the package.

Twelve actions can be specified by a link:

Execute Menu Item—Any menu item (including the Apple Menu) can be selected using this action specifier. For instance, if a user wants to build a print button into the PDF document, the link could be set to select the Print option under the File menu.

Go To View—This action jumps the user to any particular page and magnification of the PDF document. For instance, if superscript numerals were used to reference endnotes, the link could be specified to jump to the endnote page at the appropriate location and magnification for viewing.

Import Form Data—This option would be used to import default form data from a Web server.

Movie—Specifying this action will play a QuickTime movie that is placed in the PDF document. Specific QuickTime controls pertaining to looping and movie controls can be set from this menu.

Open File—This action will open another PDF document. This is useful for very long technical manuals. It may not be practical to have a very large PDF document, but rather break it down into chapters and then link the end of the chapters with the new documents.

Read Article—Specifying this action will bring up a window of readable articles within the document.

Reset Form—Clears all data previously entered into a form. This option is useful if a *Reset* button is designated in the form.

Show/Hide Field—Will show or hide any fields that may occur within the PDF document.

Sound—Lets the user designate a sound to be played upon link activation. As with movies, the sound is not embedded in the PDF file, only a location reference to the sound file is saved.

Submit Form—Any data that has been placed into a form will be submitted to the specified URL when this link is activated. *(See Creating Forms for more detail.)*

World Wide Web Link—This link jumps the user to a specified Web page. For the jump to occur, the user must have internet access and have a Web browser configured to work with Acrobat.

Creating Forms

Since Web publishing is the prevailing buzz, Acrobat provides a tool for interactive data submission over the Internet via the PDF format.

Forms creation in Acrobat 3.0 is something of a misnomer—it should more appropriately be titled "data field definition" because the look of the form is done in the original page-layout application or scanned directly to PDF format.

The concept behind forms is simple. Any document can be created containing boxes for certain types of data or end-user input. That document can then be converted into a PDF document and using the forms function of Exchange, those data fields can be described and defined.

Exchange let users add functions like radio buttons, check boxes, text entry fields, list boxes, and other options which could be set to collect data over the Web via PDF.

The forms function would add great value for an employer who would want to post a PDF-version of its employment application on the Web. Like any paper document with check boxes for gender, text entry for address, and perhaps a list of job titles, the PDF application could have those functions built into it.

After the data had been entered on the user end, a button to submit the data could be added to the PDF, and a CGI-script on the Web server could collect and sort the submitted data. The forms function essentially allows the interactivity of HTML to be built into a PDF document.

Creating Notes

Similar to those sticky Post-It notes you put all over your office, Exchange allows you to apply notes directly on the page. Notes are a great way to add comments or bring attention to an area of interest on a specific page. To create a note:

1. Select the note icon from the tool bar.
2. A crosshair appears. Drag a box to the size you wish the note to be.
3. The note will appear, and the flashing cursor allows you to begin typing.
4. The name and color of the note can be changed by double clicking on the note's title bar. *When the title bar is double clicked, a Note Properties pop-up window will appear allowing these changes to be made. Note preferences can also be set in the Notes preferences pop-up window under File, Preferences.*
5. The note can be closed by clicking the box in the upper left corner.
6. Once the note is closed, it can be reopened and read or edited by double clicking on the closed note icon.

Editing

The editing of PDF documents is available on a document level basis and a content-level basis. The document level includes features to:

- Move pages
- Copy pages
- Delete pages
- Replace pages
- Rotate pages
- Crop pages

Notes icon

Closed note

Amie
This is what a note looks like when created in Acrobat Exchange.
The note can be sized, and the color can be changed by double clicking on the title bar.
The note can be closed by clicking on the box in the upper left corner. And it can be reopened by double clicking on the note icon.

Open note

Content level editing features include text touch-ups, provided the font has been embedded. Touch Up options include:

- Character color
- Character size
- Character placement

Document Level Editing

One of the chief advantages of the PDF format over its PostScript parent is page independence. The pages of a Post-Script file cannot be separated within the file. PDF files are logically structured so that each page is individually defined and extractable.

Move, Copy, Delete, Replace Pages

Page independence functionality allows individual pages of the PDF document to be moved, copied, deleted, or replaced within a file. Pages can also be inserted from other PDF documents. This ability allows for the customization of PDF documents. For example, a PDF instruction manual could be customized for an individual product model, while still including all of the general information common to the entire product line. This type of customized service could be accomplished on a print or on-line, on-demand basis.

The best way to move pages around is in the *Thumbnails view*. Not only can you view the pages in succession, but they are easy to grab and move as one entity due to their size.

Move Pages

Moving pages is useful when restructuring the page order of a document.

1. *Thumbnails view* should be selected from the *View* menu.
2. Select the hand tool and click and hold on the thumbnail page number (a small page icon appears attached to the arrow cursor).
3. Drag the thumbnail to the destination of choice and a black line will appear between the already existing page order. *This line represents the placement of the page which is about to be made.*
4. Release the mouse and the thumbnail is placed in the new order as is the page itself.

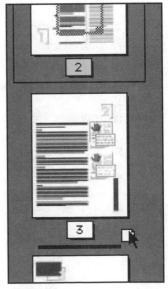

Moving Pages

The PDF thumbnails will reflow and will be renumbered if necessary.

Copy Pages

Pages may be copied within a document, or they may be copied from one document and inserted in another. To copy pages within a document:

1. *Thumbnails view* option should be selected.
2. Select the hand tool and click and hold on the thumbnail page number (a small page icon appears attached to the arrow cursor)
3. Hold down the *Option* key. A "+" appears on the small page icon.
4. Drag the thumbnail to the destination of choice and a black line will appear between the already existing page order. *This line represents the placement of the page which is about to be made.*
5. Release the mouse and the thumbnail is placed in the new order as is the page itself.

Copying Pages

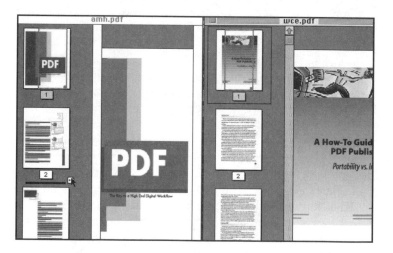

Copying Pages between documents

To copy pages from one document to another:

1. Open both documents with *Thumbnails view* selected.
2. Select *Tile Vertically* or *Tile Horizontally* from the *Window* menu.
3. Select the hand tool and click and hold on the thumbnail

page number which is being copied (a small page icon appears attached to the arrow cursor).

3. Drag the thumbnail to the point of destination in the other document.

4. A black line will appear between the already existing page order. *This line represents the placement of the page which is about to be made.*

5. Release the mouse and the thumbnail is placed in the new order as is the page itself.

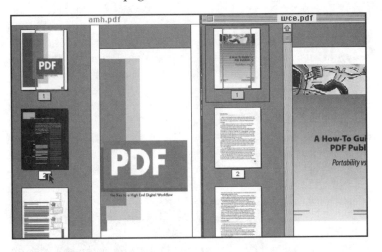

Replace Pages

Replace Pages

Pages may also be copied from one document and inserted into another document, replacing a page. This may be important for extensive document changes or additions such as the example of the PDF instruction manual. Instead of going back to the original application file, making changes or additions, and distilling again, just the changed or added pages can be distilled and added to the first PDF. To replace a page:

1. Open both documents with *Thumbnails view* selected.

2. Select *Tile Vertically* or *Tile Horizontally* from the *Window* menu.

3. Select the hand tool and click and hold on the thumbnail page number which is being copied (a small page icon appears attached to the arrow cursor)

4. Drag the thumbnail directly on top of the page number icon of the thumbnail which you intended to replace.

5. The page being replaced will be highlighted in black.

6. Release the mouse and the thumbnail is replaced.

The page will be deleted, but the memory allotment will still exist. In order to solve this problem, you must Save As to remove the extraneous data.

Delete Pages

Simply select delete pages from the Document window. A pop-up window will ask you which pages you wish to delete. Another pop-up window will follow asking if you are sure you want to delete these pages. If you're sure, click *Yes* and the page will be deleted.

Crop Pages

Unlike conventional cropping, either digital or analog, which removes and deletes the data, Exchange only removes the material from the visible page. Thus, all cropping changes can be undone. Even if a *Save As* is applied to a cropped page within the PDF, the original page information can be retrieved by going back into the *Crop* dialog box and reducing the margins to 0 in all directions.

Crop pages allows the cropping of the page borders to any specified length. To crop a page:

1. Open the file you wish to crop.

2. Select *Crop Pages...* from the Document Window on the main menu bar.

3. A pop-up window appears. Make the necessary margin and page selections.

4. Press OK.

Crop Pages

Rotate Pages

Exchange allows you to rotate pages within in a PDF document. All pages or individual pages can be rotated either clockwise or counterclockwise in 90-degree increments. It is not possible to rotate arbitrarily.

Content Level Editing

Another significant advantage of the Portable Document Format is the retention of vector-based information. This means that when fonts are embedded, the actual outlines are preserved, keeping them in a semi-editable state.

Text Touch-ups

Probably the most common user misconception about the PDF format is in regards to its editability. Unlike other document formats (i.e., native Quark, Microsoft Word or PageMaker formats), the objects that make up the PDF document cannot be moved, deleted or altered. For the most part, PDF documents are locked, page independent, data containers that can be viewed, searched and printed. Pages as entire entities can be moved around, but the contents within cannot.

There is some editability available within Exchange, and this some may be all you need. However it's crucial to understand the limitations of that editability. Acrobat provides two tools for text selection.

Keep in mind that changing characters with the Text touch-up tool cannot be done to fonts that have been subsetted. If you foresee the need for text revisions, then be safe and Embed All fonts when distilling the file.

Select Text Tool

The Select Text tool allows for text to be highlighted and copied to another application program as ASCII text. This function is very similar to the text copy functions of most other applications. To select text:

Select Text

The *Select Text* tool allows text to be
highlighted and copied to another
application if allowed by the security features of Acrobat. See Security
later in this chapter.

Selecting text

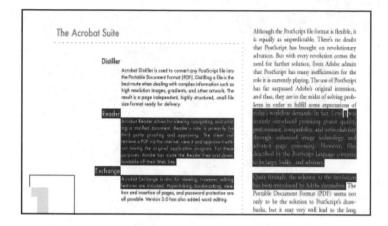

1. Click on the *Select Text* tool in the Menu Bar or under the
   Tools menu.
2. A cursor will appear. Highlight the text you wish to copy.
3. Select *Copy* from the *Edit* menu.
4. Paste in the text into any application.

The *Text Select* tool will select text on a line-by-line basis. If text
was originally flowed into separate text boxes, then the text
select tool, as shown above, may select text you do not wish to
include. To select a specific portion such as a paragraph:

1. Click on the Select Text tool in the Menu Bar or under the
   Tools menu.
2. Hold down *Option* key, and a dotted box will appear over
   the cursor.
3. The cursor will allow you to drag a selection box over the
   text you wish to select.
4. The text within the box will become highlighted.
5. Select *Copy* from the *Edit* menu.
6. Paste the text into any application.

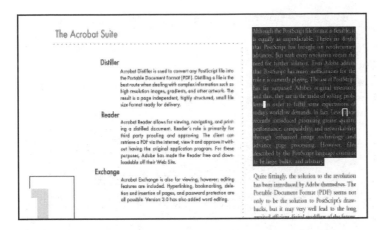

Selecting a portion of text

Text Touch-up Tool

The *Text Touch-Up* tool offers limited text changes on a line-by-line basis given certain criteria. For instance,

- To change characters in a line, the font used for the text must either be available on your computer or the full font must be embedded within the PDF document. *(See font embedding in Chapter 5).*
- If the font used on the text is an embedded subset, character changes will not be allowed.

To determine how a font is embedded in a PDF document, select *Document Info, Fonts* under the *File* menu. This dialog box will identify fonts used and how they were embedded.

If the text can be edited, it can only be done on a line-by-line basis because Acrobat can't reflow text through a document. However, to fix a last minute price change in a digital ad or a misspelled word in a lengthy document makes the Touch-up tool a valuable asset.

In addition, *Text Touch-Up* provides other features such as applying color to text and scaling. To apply a *Text Touch-up*:

1. Select the *Text touch-ups* icon on the tool bar.
2. Place the cursor where you want to edit the text.
3. A box appears outlining the line of text.
4. Highlight the text you plan to edit.
5. Select *Text Attributes* from the *Edit* menu.

The Text Touch-Up tool allows for small type changes to be made to PDF documents. The availability and functionality of this tool is limited by a number of factors.

recently introduced promising greater quality, performance, compatibility, and networkability through enhanced image technology and advance page processing. However, files described by the PostScript language continue to be large, bulky, and arbitrary.

Quite fittingly, the solution to the revolution has been introduced by Adobe themselves. The Portable Document Format (PDF) seems not

At this point, a floating pallette appears with choices for *Font, Character, and Line*.

Font

The text editing options of the Text Touch-up Tool are broken down into three sections. The options are
- Font selection
- Size
- Fill color
- Outline color.

Text Touch-Up Font Options

If the font size is increased over the length of the line, the copy will flow off the page and will not be viewable, so be careful when enlarging font size.

The Font option in Text Touch-Up is useful for adding color to links or highlights after the PDF file has been created.

Character

The character options include the traditional PostScript controls for typographic manipulation and formatting—scaling, letterspacing and word spacing.

Text Touch-Up Character Options

Any changes that affect the line length, and force the copy off the page will not be viewable.

Line

The line options handle the alignment of the line being edited. Flush left, center, flush right and justify are the options available at this level. The two measurements at the bottom affect the placement of the text line from either the left or right page border. For instance, a value of zero entered in the left-side box will place the left edge of the line on the edge of the page.

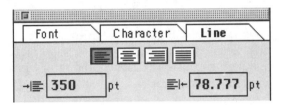

Text Touch-Up Line Options

Security

Exchange also contains options for insuring PDF security. On the broadest level, a password can be set to open the PDF document. More specifically, printing, changing the document, selecting text and graphics, adding or changing notes and form field entry can all be controlled with a password.

To set security options, select *Save As* under the File Menu and click on the *Security...* button. A dialog box will appear and all of the functions can be set there.

```
┌─────────────────────────────────────────────┐
│ ┌ Specify Password To ──────────────────────┐ │
│                                              │
│   Open the Document:        [ •••• ]         │
│                                              │
│   Change Security Options:  [ ••••• ]        │
│                                              │
│ ┌ Do Not Allow ─────────────────────────────┐ │
│   ⊠ Printing                                 │
│   ⊠ Changing the Document                    │
│   ⊠ Selecting Text and Graphics             │
│   ⊠ Adding or Changing Notes and Form Fields │
│                                              │
│              ( Cancel )  ‖ OK ‖              │
└─────────────────────────────────────────────┘
```

Acrobat's Extendibility

One of the most interesting functions possible with PDF is that third party developers have the ability to write plug-ins to extend Acrobat's capability. There are many commercially created plug-ins available for handling text in PDF files, but there are currently no plug-ins available which directly support high-end printing production like printing color separations of PDF files. Adobe is developing a plug-in that will allow both process and spot plates to be printed as well as custom settings for screen angles, halftone dot shapes and color rendering. The intention of this plug-in is to show the possibilities that PDF can give high-end users and encourage third party developers to supply further functions.

Extended Print Services, the plug-in (now in beta) tested for this book, offers another dialog box along with "Print" under the File menu. The dialog box is an extended version of the print dialog box divided into four parts—Document, Pages, Output and Color

Document

This part is basically the normal print dialog box with the general settings of page range, number of copies and PPD selection. It is also possible to save all the settings that are used and reload them later.

Pages

The Pages option includes the settings that are normally found in Page Setup like media size and orientation.

Output

Output controls let the user choose to reduce the size of the page (usually found in Page Setup), but the image can be scaled anamorphically which would be practical for flexographic printing. Also included in the Output options are Printers Marks, Mirror and Negative options.

Color

Producing color separations is the heart of what PDF must do to be a viable part of the high-end publishing workflow. And the Color options are where it's done. The first option is how the color output (screen angles, dot shapes, UCR levels) should be controlled. There are three main choices: either the printer's default setting, the document's setting, or both these can be overridden by the settings specified in the dialog box. Next the file can be printed either as a composite page or as separations. Screening control allows the halftone frequency, dot shape and screen angles to be set to the PPD-defined defaults or to custom levels. If the printer has Color Rendering Dictionaries installed, different rendering intents can also be specified from within the Color option dialog box.

The beta-version of Extended Print Services is a demonstration that shows the functionality that can be added to Exchange and PDF. Third-party developers will create plug-ins that will duplicate, and perhaps expand upon, the capabilities just described.

Reader

Reader is the baby brother or sister in the Acrobat family—definitely a part of the family, but you don't want to let them play with your toys. This is to say that Reader can view, navigate, search and print PDF documents. It can also enjoy any of the interactivity built-in to PDF documents through Exchange like Web-links and QuickTime movies. However, that's about the limit of what Reader can do. It cannot touch-up text, add interactivity, or make page-level changes like cropping. Anything that might change the structure of the PDF file can't be accomplished in Reader.

And, it's not designed to do those functions. Adobe markets Reader as "The free viewing companion to Acrobat . . .". It is designed to be a freely distributable way to share PDF documents across different platforms. It is available on all three major platforms—Macintosh, Windows and UNIX.

Capabilities

Reader ia a great way to soft proof, and it's the simplest way to view PDF files downloaded from the Web. Files can be viewed and printed, but they cannot be edited in any way. Reader does not have any saving capabilities. Text can be selected, copied, and pasted into another application but touch-ups can not be applied. Basically, it's a "look, but don't change" application.

Reader can view Notes, but they can't be edited. This means that responses or further comments cannot be added to a preexisting note using Reader. Reader also supports searching through the Find command which further enhances the use of Reader as a viewing program.

Why Use Reader?

Reader does have some advantages and is actually a good choice in some situations. If you are a designer sending a menu design to a restaurant for approval, Reader is efficient. Simply save the file as a PDF (as explained in Chapter 5) and send it to the restaurant client via E-mail. The client does not have to invest in Exchange just to view the menu. Reader is free and easy to download directly from Adobe's Web site. The expense of printing proofs and the dependency on making that express mail pickup is no longer necessary either. The client can view the menu in full color on screen at virtually no cost on either end.

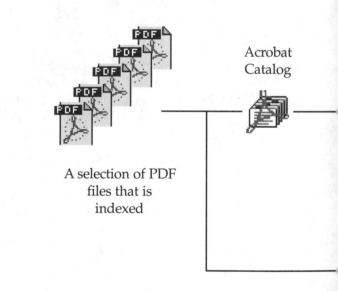

Acrobat Catalog

A selection of PDF files that is indexed

This is also a great example of an instance where you would want no editability in your digital document. You, the designer, would not be interested in your client moving images or changing fonts. Notes can be viewed, so if you wanted to include a few questions or concerns in need of consideration, Reader will allow the client to access these notes. Comments cannot be directly added on the client end, but after all, the file is being E-mailed, so comments can attached as with regular mail.

Adobe Acrobat Catalog and Search
Files and the information contained within them are only as valuable as the ability to access that information. What good is information if it is buried deep within a file? Currently there is no direct and effective way to store and retrieve files created in any one of today's application programs. Acrobat's solution to the archival prospect lies within the Catalog and Search features in the Acrobat suite. Catalog is a stand-alone application, while Search is a plug-in packaged with Reader and Exchange.

The index file of the cataloged PDF files

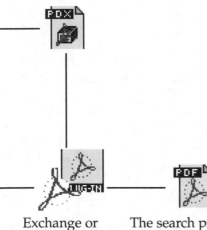

Exchange or Reader with the Acrobat search plug in

The search pinpoints the PDF files that match the search criteria

Catalog and Search Market

Anyone who needs to manage large volumes of PDF documents or wants to have instant access to specific portions of files will benefit from using Catalog and Search. Grouping all files and indexing them is an advantage which will lead to more streamlined workflows and will significantly decrease downtime in the location of files and images. The implementation of an index with searching capability for archiving is a necessary part of digital workflow. Since storage space is so expensive and digital workflows for printers are evolving and incorporating the usage of PDF files, direct archival storage in a structured manner is needed.

How Does it Work?

Similar to a filing cabinet, hundreds of individual documents can be grouped together in one location. This is called indexing and is possible through the use of Acrobat Catalog. But unlike the old file cabinet setup, documents can found easily. Not only can they be found by name or author, they can also be accessed by one word or phrase buried deep within the document. This function is called searching and is possible when using Acrobat Search. So, if you want to rid the office of those stacks of paper documents and those bulky file cabinets, or you have trouble finding the one piece of paper you're looking for, Catalog and Search are worthwhile options.

The Planning Stage in Exchange

Prior to index building in Catalog and while the PDF is still in Exchange, there are several options which should be specified in order to ensure indexing efficiency. The most important areas of concern are:

- Document information box options
- Thumbnails/bookmarks
- Optimizing
- Notes

Document Information Box

Access to the dialog box in Exchange is found in the File menu, Document Info, General menu. The dialog box which appears is the key to all category searching. This box allows the user to specify document information such as title, subject, author and keywords. Defining these fields allows Catalog to more efficiently indexed PDF files

```
╔═══════════════ General Info ═══════════════╗
║                                            ║
║   Filename:  Snoopy:Desktop Folder: mxw.pdf║
║                                            ║
║      Title: │Portable Document Format: Applications for Business│
║                                            ║
║    Subject: │Direct PDF applications for offices│
║                                            ║
║     Author: │Mark Witkowski│               ║
║                                            ║
║   Keywords: │Portable Document Format PDF Archiving│
║                                            ║
║     Creator: Not Available                 ║
║    Producer: Acrobat Distiller 3.0 for Macintosh
║                                            ║
║     Created: 11/19/96 4:40:16 PM           ║
║    Modified: 1/15/97 3:01:32 PM            ║
║                                            ║
║   Optimized: Yes        File Size: 105297 Bytes
║                                            ║
║              [ Cancel ]    [  OK  ]        ║
╚════════════════════════════════════════════╝
```

PDF Document Info Window

The Document Information box is probably the most overlooked step in the process, and it is actually the most essential for archiving purposes. The choices should be completed in a similar manner for all files being indexed.

Thumbnails and Bookmarks
The prior creation of thumbnails and bookmarks in Exchange, will help searchers navigate through the document after the "hits" are located. When a user is directed to a "hit" on the page, the reading typically does not end there. Since you have full access to the entire document, thumbnails and bookmarks serve as an effective and necessary navigation tool, especially if the document being searched is lengthy.

Remember that if thumbnails and bookmarks are to be utilized in Catalog and Search, they must be created prior to indexing in Exchange.

Optimizing
Optimization of a file is an important operation to perform on all PDF documents that are going to be cataloged. An optimized file is more efficiently structured allowing Reader or Exchange better access to the objects in the file.

Byte-serving — Aims at reducing file download times by only allowing single page transfers Also produces quicker screen re-draw times by first displaying approximations of fonts, then replaces them later on.

Storage Locations
Once the PDF files are properly prepared in Exchange, they should be saved to a dedicated folder in which all the files being

Notes are electronic annotations which are included on the screen view, but do not print out. Unfortunately, the notes contained within the files in the index are not searchable.

indexed will go. Further sub grouping of these files at this point will allow separate more specific indexes made for large volumes od PDF files. This will enable searchers to more accurately pinpoint queries later.

Pre-sorting large amounts of related files, and/or the breaking up of all extremely large singular files enables quicker, more directed searching. The creation of a structured organization and naming system will further streamline the searching function. You do want fast searching.

Using Acrobat Catalog

When Catalog is first opened the screen looks very similar to Distiller. The first step after opening Catalog is to immediately check and set the preferences. The preferences set at this point are kept every time subsequent indexes are built. If you are rebuilding an existing index, it will use the preferences set at the time of the re-build. These preferences may not necessarily be the ones used in the original build. It is necessary to determine the end use of the index when setting the preferences because these settings affect the later uses of the index.

The preferences menu is found under the Edit menu. It consists of five sections:
- Index
- Index Defaults
- Logging
- Drop Folders
- Custom Fields

Index

Purging is the deletion of the entire index and all of its contents. When an index is purged all of the files are irretrievably erased.

The index box contains several settings regarding the index in general. The Purge time is a setting which delays the purge or deletion of an index. The default time setting is 15 minutes. This time span will allow users who may be using the index on a network to complete their searches before the index begins erasing.

Catalog Preferences Window

The *Document Section Size* is the threshold at which Acrobat will cutoff large documents and segment them into as many parts as specified. For instance, if the size is set to 250,000 words, and a file containing 300,000 words is indexed, it will be cut off at 250,000 words and a second index file will be created including the remaining 50,000 words. The intention of this is to keep the catalog and search functions operating quickly.

Choosing the group size for CD-ROM allows Acrobat to cut off the size of the singular index to specified limitations for use on CD storage media. There is a limit and ideal format for CD-ROM storage. It is important for CD creation that particular attention be paid to this setting.

Making indexes available after partial completion is best used when indexing large amounts of information. The smaller the number in this field, the faster viewing and usage of the completed parts of the index. If large amounts of data are being cataloged, it is wise to set the value in this field to a low number so that users have access to at least some information.

Setting the *Index Cache Size* to larger values will allow faster index build times on a Macintosh.

Checking the box to allow indexing on a separate drive is not recommended if there is ever a possible future for cross platform use of the index. The separate drive feature is only allowed on the Macintosh platform, not on the Windows platform.

The DOS-compatible folder names is also important for cross-platform functions. When this box is checked, the computer limits the naming of files to the least common denominator—which is MS DOS names.

Index Defaults

The choices made in this section pertain to the limiting factors of the index. The choices also determine the functionality of the search. Selecting or deselecting each feature in this box can reduce the overall size of the index approximately 10 to 15 percent for each option. It is important to note that with these choices you are sacrificing storage space for functionality in the search process. It is the relationship between functionality and space that becomes a focal point for the selections made.

On a Macintosh platform you have the ability to index files on different drives, but on a DOS platform all files must be in the same drive. It is recommended that all files regardless of platform be included within the same folder, and on the same drive.

If you are working on a Macintosh platform and plan to transfer this index at any time to a MS-DOS platform, it is important to keep all file names in accordance to MS-DOS standards. Character names must be no longer than eight ASCII characters with a three character extension. Example: acrobat.pdf— "acrobat" is the file name and ".pdf" is the extension.

146

If CD-ROM storage is a possibility, now or in the future, it is important to check the *Optimize for CD-ROM* box. This option organizes the data in an order that is ideal for CD storage and retrieval, especially for older 2X and 4X CD-Readers.

The only absolutely necessary consideration that must always be checked is the *Add IDs to Acrobat 1.0 PDF files.* This will add a tag to PDF files created before PDF version 1.2. This tag will let Catalog recognize the PDF 1.0 and 1.1 files and will include them in the field.

Depending on the desired user pool of the index, the choices in *Word options* should differ. If several users needing broad searching capabilities will be using the index, options for: Case sensitive, Sounds Like, and Word Stemming should all be enabled. However, if a select group of users who know exactly what they are looking for are using the index, these options may not need to be included.

```
╔══════════════ Catalog Preferences ══════════════╗
║  ┌──────────┐  ┌─Logging──────────────────────┐  ║
║  │   Index  │  │ ⊠ Enable Logging             │  ║
║  │          │  │    ⊠ Log Search Engine Messages │ ║
║  │Index Defaults│ □ Log Compatability Warnings │  ║
║  │          │  │                              │  ║
║  │  Logging │  │ Maximum Log File Size: 1024 Kilobytes │ ║
║  │          │  │                              │  ║
║  │Drop Folders│ Log File Name: Catalog Log File │  ║
║  │          │  │                              │  ║
║  │Custom Fields│ Save Log File In: Index Folder ▼ │ ║
║  │          │  │ Custom Folder:               │  ║
║  │          │  │              [ Choose... ]   │  ║
║  [ Defaults ]    [ Cancel ]  [ OK ]              ║
╚══════════════════════════════════════════════════╝
```

Log files are good feedback tools from the index. Information shedding light on the way in which the created index is working and how often the index is used can be provided.

Logging

Logging creates a report file which contains all information when indexes are built and records the status after building.

Choices include having the log file updated every time there is an inquiry with the search engine. You can set the name and destination of the log file created at this stage. Even though the log file will be recognizable, it is a file name relative to the index which will insure correlation to that index. The destination of the report file should be in the folder containing the index and related files. The information in the report file which is a Simple Text file includes time stamp and a message report. You can set the maximum size of the file so that it gets deleted and reset at a certain point.

Drop Folders
These settings determine the default index name and designate where the peripheral files will be created for the index. It is important to remember that all files for a particular index should be contained in one folder to eliminate confusion in the future. Taking these steps now will add to the longevity of the index.

Custom Fields
The creation of information fields for custom versions of Acrobat are created at this box. The declaration of integer, text and string data fields can be specified at this point. This feature is supported by custom versions of Acrobat.

Building the Index
The actual building of the index is a relatively simple task now that all files are set up in a structured manner. It is at this stage that many of the important planning steps taken will help shape the index.

```
┌─────────────────────────────────────────────────┐
│▒▒▒▒▒▒▒▒▒▒▒▒▒▒▒ Index Definition ▒▒▒▒▒▒▒▒▒▒▒▒▒▒▒▒│
│ Index File:                          ┌─────────┐ │
│                                      │  Save   │ │
│                                      └─────────┘ │
│                                      ┌─────────┐ │
│                                      │ Save As…│ │
│ Index Title:  ┌──────────────────┐   └─────────┘ │
│               │Your title here   │   ┌─────────┐ │
│ Index Description:                   │ Cancel  │ │
│ ┌────────────────────────────────┐   └─────────┘ │
│ │Description of the index here.  │⇧             │
│ │Remember only 250 characters in │   ┌─────────┐ │
│ │this box!                       │   │ Options │ │
│ │                                │⇩  └─────────┘ │
│ └────────────────────────────────┘   ┌─────────┐ │
│                                      │  Build  │ │
│ ┌Include Directories─────────────┐   └─────────┘ │
│ │                                │⇧  ┌─────────┐ │
│ │                                │   │  Add…   │ │
│ │                                │   └─────────┘ │
│ │                                │⇩  ┌─────────┐ │
│ └────────────────────────────────┘   │ Remove  │ │
│                                      └─────────┘ │
│ ┌Exclude Directories─────────────┐   ┌─────────┐ │
│ │                                │⇧  │  Add…   │ │
│ │                                │   └─────────┘ │
│ │                                │⇩  ┌─────────┐ │
│ └────────────────────────────────┘   │ Remove  │ │
│                                      └─────────┘ │
└─────────────────────────────────────────────────┘
```

Where to Begin Indexing

With Acrobat Catalog running, select new from the file menu. The Index Definition dialog box that appears controls everything that index will contain, as well as its file name and description.

1. Name the index
2. Give a summary of the index. *There is a maximum of 250 characters in this box, so be concise, but descriptive.*
3. Choose the folders that will be included in the index.
4. Click on the *Add* button. A document selection box will appear. In order to select an entire folder, click on the bar at the bottom of the box which starts with select. This is where the careful planning of folders and sub folders becomes important.

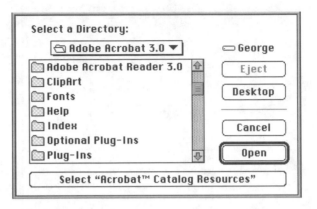

Now that the files are chosen,

5. Click on the *Options* button. The most important part of this box is the selection of stop words, or words that should be included in the index. Choosing words that will not appear in the index can have a significant impact on the index size. For instance, words such as: *and*, *the*, or *for* are not necessarily needed and can be cut out in order to reduce the index size. The choices made in this box are specific only to this particular index, and are used whenever that index is updated.

Use the Save button in the index definition box for updating the information to an existing index definition.

6. Click on *Save as*. Now that the overall index has been set in the Index Definition box, the *Save as* dialog box allows you to give the central index definition a file name. The

index file should be saved in the master folder previously set up with the PDF files. Choosing the *Add to Index to Schedule* is the only choice left to make if you want to add the index to the automatic rebuild schedule. Once everything is set, click on the save button. This will create a central index definition file with a .pdx extension.

7. Under the Index menu choose the *Build* option to do the actual building of the index. Once inside the build feature you will be at a file selection dialogue box. To build an index, highlight the index definition file (with a .pdx extension) you want, then on the open button, then let Catalog do its work. When the actual index is built, a series of nine folders are created to support the central index definition. Depending on the amount of text and graphics contained in the pages, cataloging times may vary. For more text, allow longer times for building.

Maintenance

After the index is first built, your work is not done. It is important to keep the index and its contents up to date. Periodic rebuilding of the index and additions are necessary. This is very easily done.

1. The first step is placing the new PDF files into the desired index folders. In Catalog select *Build* from the index menu. Then select the index file with the .pdx extension.
2. If there are no changes to the overall setup to the index, just click *Build* and the index will be updated and include the new files.

Major Rebuilds

If there have been significant changes to files in the index or many new files have been added or options have changed, then purging and rebuilding the index is necessary. Purging erases all information in the existing index. The purge function is found in the *Build* menu, and should only be used when complete changes need to be made to the index. After the index has been purged, the previously outlined rebuild techniques can be followed.

Purge and rebuild indexes that have been rebuilt several times. This is because each time you rebuild an index it gets a little bit larger. Purging this index will reclaim disk space and make searching quicker.

Remember: you can add an index to a schedule menu when you are in the Save as box of the index definition.

Scheduling

In order for a streamlined service of the rebuilding process, the Schedule feature needs to be enabled. Scheduling will allow automatic updating of the index. This feature should be used if the catalog is being constantly updated and renovated.

1. The first step in the schedule build setup is to access the *Schedule Builds* dialog box. Go under the index menu to the schedule option.

2. Once inside the *Schedule Builds* box, select the indexes you want to add to the schedule. Use the same techniques outlined earlier for selecting indexes.

3. Decide how often you want the indexes to be built: *Continuously, once,* or *on a set time schedule.* Ideally, you want to rebuild the indexes when no one is using the index. You can set the time of rebuild to be overnight so it does not interfere with anyone's searching.

The drawback to the schedule tool is that the computer system must be running 24 hours a day 7 days a week. If there is any interruption either in electricity or manual switching, the schedule must be re-defined and re-started.

Acrobat Search

Acrobat Search is a plug-in supplied with Exchange and Reader.

Search preferences must be set before you do your first search. It is a relatively easy task to change and redefine the preferences in this menu. Settings for queries, results, highlighting and indexes can be set.

Setting Search Preferences

The Acrobat Search Preferences dialog box can be found under the File menu, Preferences, Search. The check boxes found give the flexibility to customize the way the search reports hits. Results can be organized by a host of categories.

1. Go to the Search Preferences dialog box.

2. Select how much of the query box you want users to see:
   - *Show Fields*: will choose whether or not to show document information fields
   - *Show Date*: shows or hides *with date information* box.
   - *Show Options*: enables options set in Catalog such as sounds like, word stemming etc.

3. The *Hide on Search* check box refers to keeping the Acrobat Search window open or closed after the search is done. Checking this box will hide the window when the search reports back.

4. The order in which results of a search are displayed can be set in the results option field. Several options are available for sorting returned hits. *Choose the one that best suits your needs.* You can further limit the number of returned documents at this point. Also, you can click on the *Hide on View* box to hide the results box when you view a document.

5. Highlighting the hits on a page can be set in the highlight box. Highlighting by page, word or no highlights at all can be chosen. Page highlighting is the default value.

6. Automounting servers in the indexes area will automatically mount all available indexes available when starting a search. This function is only available on a Macintosh platform.

Performing the Search

Now that all of the preferences have been set, it is finally time to perform the search. To get to the Search dialogue box, go to the Tools menu, Search, Query.

Using the Search Box

Using the Search Box is where you make the choices of where and what you want to search. The search engine does the rest of the work and reports back to you via a hit list dialog box.

1. The first step is to decide where you want to search. Click on the *Indexes* button. You will be brought to a box where you can select or deselect indexes. The sensible division and sub-division of created indexes becomes important at this point. If an index you want to search does not appear in the box, des-elect any index currently in the box and click on the add but-ton. This will bring you to a box which allows you to find your index. When you find it click on the open button. After all indexes appear in the Index Selection box, click OK.

2. Now that you have decided where to search, you must decide what to search. There are several ways to drive the search engine. First, determine what options you want to include in the search, such as:
   - Word stemming
   - Sounds like
   - Thesaurus
   - Match case
   - Proximity

3. Searching for files created on, between, before or after specif-ic dates is the next set of options which must be determined. This is a useful feature because date information is automati-cally included with all documents, and is searchable.

4. Performing searches in the "With Document Info" area is where the document information box becomes vital. The fields in this area consist of the information provided in the planning stages of the index. Each of these fields can be used to perform a search within that particular field across the selected indexes. As you can see the proper and consistent information provided in these fields is invaluable at this point.

5. The final method for searching documents is the straight text calls made in the *Find Results Containing Text* field. Several methods and options exist for narrowing or expanding these specific searches. Wildcard, boolean, phrase and comparison searching can be performed. This type of search uses typical protocols for the usage of these operators.

This icon can also be used to access the search query box.

If Automount Servers is not select-ed in the preferences box, then either click on this button, or mount them by going into the tools search, index menu item.

Explanation of Search restric-tions and options.

Word Stemming: *returns words with the same stem or root as the query word.*

Sounds Like: *returns words which may be spelled differently (incorrect spelling), but are pronounced the same as the query word.*

Thesaurus: *returns words with the same meaning as the query word.*

Match Case: *returns words which match the letters of query word in both majuscule and miniscule let-ters—upper and lowercase to non-type geeks.*

Proximity: *returns words with the boolean AND restriction to be with-in 3 pages of each another.*

Boolean operators are typed in as all capital letters:

AND: *both words.*

OR: *either or both words.*

NOT: *does not contain word.*

Wildcard: used when not sure of spelling of word, * stands for one or more characters, ? for one character.

Clicking on the Info... box will show the document information box of that file.

6. The last step in the search process is to click on the *Search* button. Acrobat Search will then access each index called for and search its text list. When it is done, it will return the list of "hits" in the order in which you set them in the preferences menu.

Search Results

Each document on this list contains the information called for in the search box. To view a file from this list either double click on it or highlight it and click on *View*.

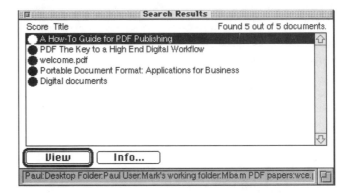

Refining a Search

An option to refine a set of returned search files can be done by re-opening the search dialog box, keying in the restraining parameters, and holding down the Option key (Macintosh) or the Control key (Windows) which will change the Search button to Refine. Click on Refine and the new requirements will be applied only to the original search results.

Word Assist

This option can almost be thought of as a pre-flight for search with the stemming, sounds like and thesaurus help functions. By using this function you can perform a mock search and see what words will be returned as *hits*. To access this box go under *Tools, Search, Word Assist*.

The Word Assist dialog box:

```
┌──────────────────────────────────────────────┐
│ ▣ ▦▦▦▦▦▦▦▦ Word Assistant ▦▦▦▦▦▦▦▦            │
│ ┌────────────────────────┐  ┌──────────────┐ │
│ Word:  │ main             │  │   Look Up    │ │
│        └────────────────────┘  └──────────────┘ │
│ Assist:│ Thesaurus        ▼ │  ┌──────────────┐ │
│        └────────────────────┘  │   Cancel     │ │
│ ┌──────────────────────┬─┐  └──────────────┘ │
│ │ capital            ⬆ │  ┌──────────────┐ │
│ │ cardinal             │  │  Indexes...  │ │
│ │ chief                │  └──────────────┘ │
│ │ dominant             │                     │
│ │ first                │                     │
│ │ foremost             │                     │
│ │ key                  │                     │
│ │ leading              │                     │
│ │ main                 │                     │
│ │ major                │                     │
│ │ outstanding          │                     │
│ │ paramount         ⬇ │                     │
│ └──────────────────────┴─┘                     │
│ │ Word assistant found 18 words.│             │
└──────────────────────────────────────────────┘
```

1. Select the indexes you want to search across is done by clicking on the indexes box. The process is now just the same as previously explained for search.

2. Choose what type of search you want to perform *Stemming, Sounds like* or *Thesaurus.*

3. Type in a word in the Word box.

4. Then click on *Search.* A list will then appear in the lower box. This list consists of words that are in the indexes chosen to search. You can then use the information from this box as a guide in your searching.

Conclusion

The usage of catalog and search features in Acrobat seem to be relatively insignificant on the surface, but in reality they are the backbone of what could be a powerful archival system. These functions are the basis for a necessary structured system to store and retrieve data.

Digital storage methods have consistently changed, as we have sought an ideal structure and format for archiving. The PDF file offers tremendous advantages and solutions over previous approaches. The efficiency and reliability that the Acrobat suite offers for archiving may very well be the answer to many concerns and problems.

It is important to realize that the construction of any storage system utilizing PDF files as the base needs to be extremely structured and well thought out. It is the planning aspects that will ultimately determine the success or failure of a system.

CHAPTER 7

PDF MARKETS & WORKFLOWS

PDF and Changing Markets

Now that we have explained how to create, view, and edit PDF files, we're going to bring it all together and discuss PDF in the job workflow environment. There's no doubt that changing customer demands are driving markets toward completely digital workflows.

Short-Run Market

Digital press technology is driving short-run, on-demand jobs, which are the ticket to the future. Printing trends are leading towards full color printing which is faster and cheaper. Entire markets have sprung up seemingly overnight. Digital color presses like the Xerox DocuColor, Agfa Chromapress and Indigo E-Print 1000 are making inroads where traditional lithography once reigned king.

Making money in printing requires keeping the presses running. This is even more true for digital color presses. In order to keep them running, data must come in a reliable self-contained package that is easy to process. Because the runs are smaller, the profit margins are very tight. To make money on 300 copies of a color brochure, the workflow must be easy-in, easy-out. The workflows must be virtually snag-less.

PDF files have the most to offer this market. No other file format can accurately render a page in such a compact and efficient manner—font formatted text, vector objects and contone images all packaged into one neat, viewable file. United Lithograph, a commercial printer in Boston, uses PDF files this way to keep its DocuColor running three shifts a day.

A PDF is a device-independent file format with good possibilities for compression. In addition, it does not "lose information" and retains the design richness. Depending on the complexity, you will most likely fit a menu in a compressed PDF file on a floppy disk. (Remember floppies?)

Designer/Printer Relationship

In order to create a seamless production environment and to best use the benefits of new press technologies, there must be an efficient exchange of files throughout the entire life of the document. Partial digital workflows have dominated the exchange of files from designer to printer for quite some time, but the results are often far from seamless.

Whether you are the designer or the printer, you have most likely witnessed some very, let's just say, less than perfect situations. For instance, how many times have you opened a file, and that horrible window appeared saying, *Fonts Missing*? How many times have you begun to preflight when you realized pictures were missing? How many times did these problems occur when the job needed to be output no later than yesterday? PDF provides the solution to these nightmares.

Currently, the majority of jobs are laid out and paginated in an application such as QuarkXPress or PageMaker. The scans are either done in-house or are sent out and placed in as FPOs. Once the designer has completed the job, the client must then approve the job. From there, the job is sent to a printer where it is trapped, imposed, proofed, approved, and printed. Since the file changes hands so many times, it is essential that the file be all inclusive and consistent. PDF may not decrease the change in hands, but it becomes the common denominator making the process easier, quicker, and more trustworthy.

Design Market

Let's create a specific scenario. Imagine that you are a designer producing a menu for a restaurant chain. You have received the photographs via FedEx, have sent them to the printer to be scanned, who in turn has supplied you with the low-res images to work with for your page layout. The menu has been designed in QuarkXPress and is ready to go to your client for approval.

How do you send the job to your client? At this stage in the game, we are past the usage of faxes. Fax requires retyping, fax quality is yukky, fax is yesterday. Since this job is four colors, the client needs a more accurate representation of the design richness. Traditionally, you would send the file together with any digital artwork and illustrations back to the printer who then opens the file, and makes sure that images are correctly linked in the OPI system. Fonts, which are (hopefully) from the same supplier and have the same set of kerning information, are loaded into the system. The prepress operator then sends the file to film, makes a proof and charges you $100 for labor and material. Even if the proof is mailed directly to your client, the entire process still takes 2–3 days.

Not only is this a tremendous hassle, but you have already added a decent chunk of money to your client's bill. After the job gets revised, and even more proofs, it becomes obvious that there must be a faster, cheaper solution.

How about PDF as a soft proof? As a designer, your job will be easier, and more importantly, you can provide a better price for your client. So, instead of sending the original application file together with pictures and illustrations to the printer for hard proofs, make a PDF file send it to your client, who can then view the job with detail and accuracy on screen.

Generating the Soft Proof
The generation of a soft proof (an on-screen proof, not hard copy) not difficult, but very crucial. PDF will be your best friend, if and only if, you distill your file correctly. For a soft proof there are several things you should play close attention to:
- Preferences in Distiller
- Font Embedding
- Compression

If there are fonts which are crucial to the look and feel of your document, or are of a large enough size that the simulated fonts will be very noticeable, make sure they are embedded. Since the file may be sent via E-mail, the size should remain as small as possible, but you do want your client to get a clear representation of the design.

Compression, especially of continuous tone images, will play a large role in the file. A 30 megabyte picture transmitted on an Internet connection of 10K per second will take fifty minutes to send. If a medium JPEG compression is applied, time will be reduced, for an average ten minute transfer.

Creating PDF soft proofs

Q: Should PDFWriter or Distiller be used to create the PDF?
A: Because the document uses EPS files and PDFWriter does not work with EPS files very well, Distiller is the best choice for creating the PDF.

Q: What compression options should be chosen?
A: Because the PDF needs to be compact to send via E-mail and is going to be viewed on screen, the images in the document should be downsampled to 72–96 dpi. JPEG medium compression could also be used to help reduce the file size.

Q: Should the fonts be embedded?
A: Chances are the client doesn't have the required fonts on the receiving computer. And since the typeface choice of the menu will carry much of the "design richness" of the document, the fonts should probably be embedded.

After the PDF file is generated, you can open it in Exchange and add notes for further description or to ask about different problems or ideas you may share with the client.

Client Approval

When the client receives the PDF file it can be opened in Acrobat Reader. Acrobat uses anti-aliasing to represent the text on screen so the overall appearance will be more realistic than just looking at a faxed copy. Images on screen are not high resolution. After the client reviews and approves the design, it's time to send the file to the printer.

Sending Final PDF for On-Demand Print

You've received approval for the menu from the client and want to send a PDF file to the print shop for reproduction. Instead of E-mail though, you are going to send the file on some type of removable media.

Q: Should PDFWriter or Distiller be used to create the PDF?
A: Again, Distiller is the best choice for creating the PDF.

Q: What compression options should be chosen?
A: Since the PDF is going to be sent via removable media, file

size is no longer critical. Instead, image quality is the deciding factor. The designer wants to insure that all of the illustrations and images in the menu reproduce at the highest possible resolution. Downsampling is probably not a good idea. However, JPEG Medium compression won't degrade image quality to unacceptable levels.

Q: Should the fonts be embedded?
A: Since this is the final output for the PDF, the designer wants to make certain that all of his/her important typeface choices make it through on the printed product. Embedding the fonts is the only option.

The work is now ready to be proofed as real images on real or almost real paper. But instead of sending the QuarkXPress files with the illustrations, you send the "okayed" PDF file to the reproduction company contact person. The reproduction company now receives the single PDF file and does not need to load the typefaces or to have your version of the creating application. Instead, Acrobat Exchange is used. From here the proof is output through the OPI system, where the low resolution images are exchanged with the high resolution versions.

The proof is as then sent back to you and for you to show the client. Of course the client will be eager to make even more corrections, but the initial soft proofs are managed with PDFs.

The Repurposing Market
Repurposing is emerging as an integral part of digital workflows. Web publishing and CD-ROM publishing become another step in addition to print media. Rather than being an alternative to print, they are complementary formats. PDF files customized for the Web or CD-ROM can be created using the same PostScript that generated a print version PDF. Through the use of the customized drop folders discussed in Chapter 5, PDF files can be customized for their intended delivery—print, Web, CD-ROM or E-mail.

If your job is Web-bound you want to make sure that download times are as short as possible. Some suggestions for setting specific compression job options in Distiller are:

File
- Acrobat 2.1 compatible

Images
- High JPEG compression for gray and color images
- Downsampling to 72 dpi for gray and color images
- CCITT Group 4 compression for monochrome line art
- Downsample monochrome line art illustrations to 300 dpi
- Convert separated CMYK images to RGB

Fonts
- Choose not to embed fonts unless they are very important to the design
- If a big headline is used, include a subset for that font

The Advertising Market

After looking at the issues for PDF and its application to the designer/printer relationship, a focus shift to yet another market segment, advertisement distribution, is in order. The distribution of advertisements is filled with different scenarios, but an overriding paranoia regarding document integrity has always been present in advertising. It is this need for integrity that led the newspaper industry to reproduce ads on films or veloxes, then physically ship them to each individual newspaper. If you are distributing to hundreds of newspapers, this can be both time-consuming and expensive.

Newspaper Advertising

Even with the onslaught of other media, newspapers still remain a potent advertising market for retailers to sell their goods and services. According to a Newspaper Association of America (NAA) report, $36 billion was spent on newspaper advertising in 1995. That figure accounts for about 22% of all money spent on advertising in 1995.

According to a 1994 study by the Sterling Resource Group, film costs for advertisers ran up to $11 for a single-color film. At that rate sending a single, full-color ad to a hundred newspapers would cost $4,400 in reproduction costs alone.

Required delivery time poses a problem for advertiser lead time. To guarantee delivery by press time, advertisers must have completed ads ready to be reproduced at least three days prior to insertion. That cuts a lot of flexibility out of their advertising message . . . especially in today's "just-in-time" business world. And on top of that, shipping ads overnight to 100 newspapers could cost over $1,000. Also, it's not a practical solution.

World Digitization

As the world began digitizing in the 1990s, advertisers and newspapers looked for a way to integrate the ad delivery process into a digital workflow. Retailers realized that they could save thousands of dollars in reproduction costs by delivering digital ads to newspapers.

Initially, advertisers began sending original application files to newspaper via removable media. However, this brought up the problem of reliability. Films and veloxes were reliable. The digital realm at this time was not.

According to the Sterling study, common problems in digital distribution included:
- Missing fonts
- Corrupt files
- Missing graphic elements
- Lack of accuracy
- Variation in application software
- Use of software extensions not available at the newspaper

Digital Growing Pains

While the entire graphic arts industry experienced these digital growing pains, the effects were especially hard on newspapers. If a printer had a problem with a digital file, s/he could reschedule the job. If a newspaper couldn't print a digital file, that revenue was lost for that edition. If the ad was about a "One-Day-Only" sale, the revenue was irrevocably lost. So, both the newspaper and the advertiser lost.

Other Digital Options

Why not send PostScript files? This is also impractical because PostScript files are generally written for a specific output device. If an advertiser has to generate customized PostScript streams for each newspaper, they might as well send films. Sending films would be more productive and certainly more reliable than sending huge customized files to newspapers. On top of file format problems, delivering the ads was still a problem, when sending veloxes or removable media. The ad still had to be shipped through expensive ground or air delivery. The newspaper industry needed a file format that was self-contained, cross-platform, reliable and compact enough to be transmitted quickly. (Can you see where this is headed?)

The PDF format provided the newspaper advertising community a reliable way to economically and quickly reproduce digital newspaper ads. With reliability, fast turnaround and cheap reproduction out of the way, inexpensive distribution became the focus. The Associated Press was the first to really tackle this issue.

AdSend

Beginning in 1993, the Associated Press began offering a digital ad delivery system to newspapers. Since most newspapers were already receiving some type of AP data, either photo or copy, why not send ads using the same distribution system? AP chose to use PDF as the file format.

The Associated Press is now sending 70,000 ads a month to newspapers in PDF form. The 955 member newspapers either print the pages directly or use the "Export to EPS" to place their ads in their pages. At peak, 2,000 ads a day are handled. Included in the AdSend workflow is a job ticket which gives the newspaper information regarding the size, placement and run dates for the ad.

While being used mostly for black-and-white ads, some retailers have used color. Boscov's, a retail-store chain centered in Reading, PA, began sending pre-separated color ads in early 1996 using Distiller 2.1. This is even more effective now because Distiller 3.0 can embed halftone screen information.

The workflow is identical to traditional workflows until output. At output, the advertiser or agency generates a PDF file instead of film. This PDF file is sent along with a job ticket and a list of selected newspapers to the AdSend site. Once received, the PDF is distributed to the desired newspapers.

Delivery Criteria

To be successful, a digital ad delivery system must be able to meet three criteria—low material and transportation costs, fast turnaround time and reliability. PDF meets all of these criteria:

- Low Material Costs: Films or veloxes are generated at the printing site instead of the distribution site.
- Low Transportation Costs: Sending data via telecommunications, be it ISDN, modem or satellite, is much cheaper than sending hundreds of overnight packages.
- Fast Turnaround: Ads can sent at the last minute and still be relatively on time.
- Reliability: Because fonts and images can be embedded, all necessary components of the available for output

PDF as a Standard for Ad Delivery?

Is PDF a standard for digital ad delivery? The answer is no, but it has the potential to become one. Currently the only ANSI and ISO standard is the TIFF/IT P1 format. TIFF/IT is also endorsed by the Digital Distribution of Advertising for Publications Association (DDAP).

Some publishers, like Time, Inc., have embraced the TIFF/IT standard. Time will accept ads in PostScript but recommends TIFF/IT. Time will not accept ads as application files.

The problem with TIFF/IT is that it is raster only. (In other words a bunch of pointless pixels.) Last minute changes are impractical and difficult. While some consider the uneditability a good thing, it can have drawbacks.

For instance, a TIFF/IT ad is sent via modem to 100 hundred newspapers with a wrong phone number in it. How do you solve the problem?
1. Edit the TIFF/IT LW file in a raster editor like Photoshop. (Sounds easy, but did you ever try it?)
2. Print films from the TIFF/IT file and have the newspapers strip in the correction.
3. Correct the mistake at the originator site and resend to all 100 newspapers.

None of the solutions are practical especially in a deadline situation. What if the same situation happened with a PDF file? Solution:
1. Open the PDF ad in Exchange and use the Text Touch-Up tool to correct the wrong phone number. Done!

TIFF/IT stands for Tag Image File Format for Image Technology. TIFF/IT files come in four flavors: LW for linework and type, CT for continuous tone images, HC for high-resolution contone information and FP for merging the previous three into a single page. Because the files offer low editability and high reliability, TIFF/IT is oftentimes referred to as "digital film."

Currently, the ANSI-sponsored Committee for Graphic Arts Technology Standards (CGATS) Subcommittee 6 is working on a standard which would utilize PDF as the delivery vehicle for digital print jobs.

As Acrobat 3.0 continues to improve, full color ads could be sent as composites and then be separated by the newspaper or exported as EPS and placed on the composite news page. In addition, Acrobat 3.0's forms capability could be used as an interface to the newspapers ad scheduling system. Ads could be delivered to a newspaper be automatically scheduled, exported as EPS files and pulled into QuarkXPress or PageMaker page templates.

The Archiving Market

How many times have you wished you hadn't trashed a file or a document? Archiving is critical for a printer. It serves as a history of completed work. After a job has been printed, it is not just thrown away. What if the client needs a reprint? In traditional workflows, archiving is storing the physical consumables such as the films or plates.

Physical Archiving

Films and plates are not only bulky, but they take up space. Stacks of films and plates pile high and soon you have rooms fully consumed by this archival method. Space is real estate and real estate is money. Since markets are driven by making money, printers are looking to digital archiving.

Digital Archiving

Digital archiving is the way to go for archiving documents that are electronically composed, as most are today. As magazines and newspapers migrate to complete electronic pagination on systems that support PostScript, they have the opportunity to create an archive of pages for printing, faxing, reprinting or viewing on the screen. The real question is what format should be stored?

Some may choose the original application file, such as Quark or PageMaker. This raises longevity concerns since application versions are constantly being upgraded. The other choice is to store the PostScript file. This can also be messy due to the huge file size and the near impossibility of editability. The main goal of archiving is to save the smallest file which can be efficiently repurposed or reprinted.

PDF Archiving
Using PDF as the storage medium for archiving print jobs allows the customer, the printer sales rep or the printer to see a history of past jobs. United Lithograph of Boston has been archiving PDF versions for use by print sales reps. The files are kept on a central server which allows the reps to view a history of jobs printed for a given client. So instead of having a huge file cabinet of printed jobs in a storeroom, the rep can access a copy of the job from his/her desk.

Other Archiving
PDF is a natural file format for archiving digital documents. They are not only predictable, but they are considerably small-er in file size than other digital options. Books in PDF form could be connected to a text retrieval system and used for research purposes. With an Acrobat-based approach, users could retrieve whole pages, with graphics in place, not just text. Reference publishers who need to keep an archive of revisable text might also want an Acrobat archive for reprints, but they would probably maintain that archive alongside an editorial database.

Changing Workflows
The series of charts on the following pages shows how the integration of PDF into current prepress workflows will streamline those workflows.

Prepress Service Bureau

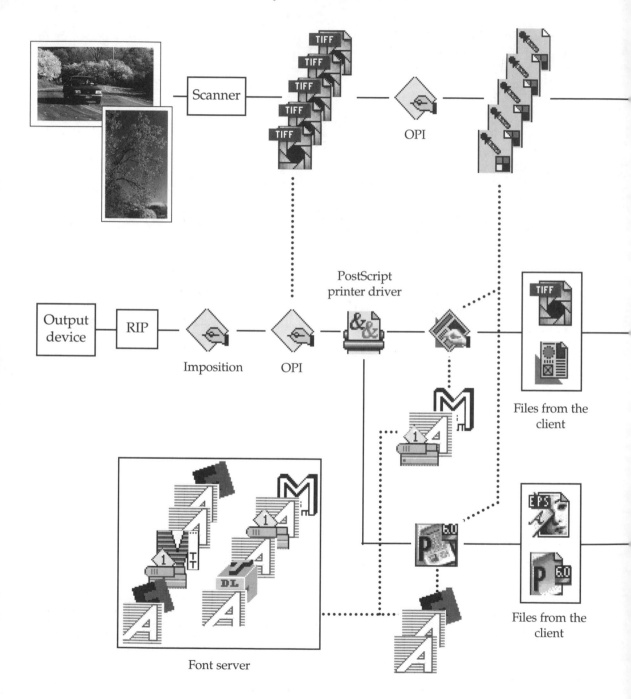

Design agencies

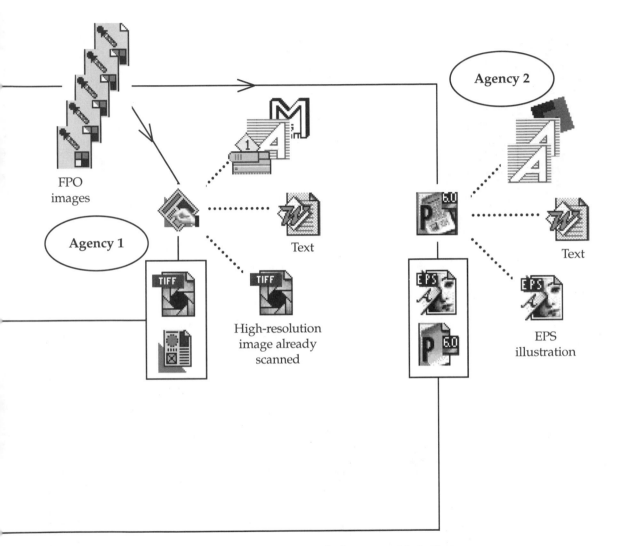

FPO
images

Agency 1

Agency 2

Text

High-resolution
image already
scanned

Text

EPS
illustration

Traditional digital prepress workflow between prepress service bureaus and their clients

Pictures are sent from clients to the reproduction company where they are scanned and placed in ther OPI server. FPO images are sent back to the clients, where they are placed into a layout program. The client may also include pictures that they have had previously scanned in high resolution (for instance, images from a previous

job). These non-FPO images together with the layout file are sent back to the reproduction company. Because of legal ramifications, fonts cannot be included. This forces the service bureau to purchase a large font library to ensure that it can meet client needs.

When the service bureau receives the

files from the client, the file is opened in the application in which the font is used, and the reproduction company's own is loaded in to the system. The job is printed through the OPI server and then sent to the RIP and imaged.

Prepress Service Bureau

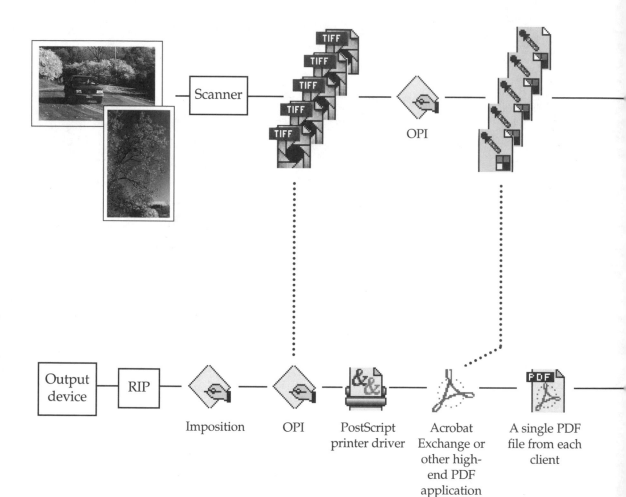

Design agencies

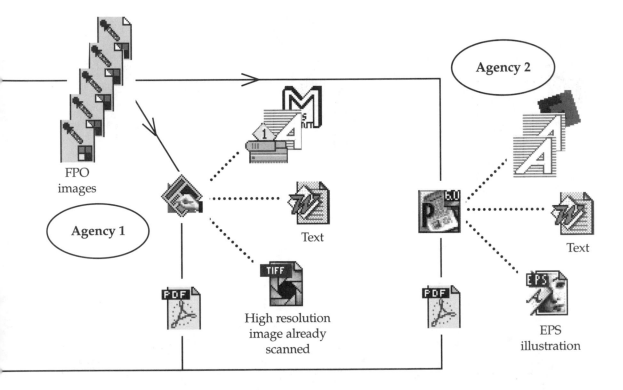

FPO
images

Agency 1

Agency 2

Text

High resolution
image already
scanned

Text

EPS
illustration

Digital prepress workflow when using PDF files.

As in the traditional workflow the reproduction company sends FPO images to the
client. The client uses the layout application of their choice. When it is time to send
the work back to the reproduction company a PDF file is generated.

Because the PDF file includes all fonts and
images, only one application-independent
file is sent.

At the reproduction company a PDF compatible print application is used, for example Acrobat Exchange, with the plug-in
Extended Print Services. From here separations can be output with registration
marks to the OPI server where the FPO
images are replaced with high-resolution
images. Further the service bureau may
use an imposition system before the data
is sent to the RIP and imaged.

Prepress Service Bureau

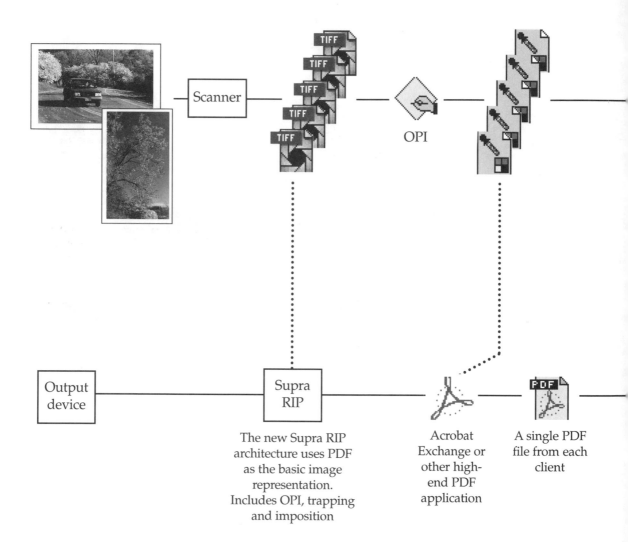

The new Supra RIP architecture uses PDF as the basic image representation. Includes OPI, trapping and imposition

Acrobat Exchange or other high-end PDF application

A single PDF file from each client

Design agencies

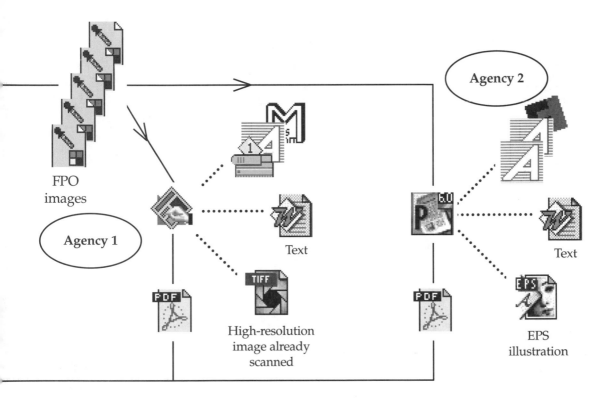

FPO
images

Agency 1

Agency 2

Text

High-resolution
image already
scanned

Text

EPS
illustration

Digital prepress workflow when using PDF files and Supra RIP

As a continuation of the PDF workflow, Adobe announced a new RIP architecture, called Supra. The major difference is that the Supra can handle both PostScript and PDF information, it actually normalizes PostScript to PDF. The new RIP architec-ture is also *multitasking* which means that several pages can be ripped simultaneous-ly. The pages can then be coordinated for imaging on a high-end output device.

CHAPTER

THE DIGITAL MARKET

As commercial (and even corporate) printing and publishing worlds migrate towards increasing reliance on digital methods, what are and where are the markets going to be? In a landmark study of digital workflow, visionary industry analyst Mills Davis predicted a new world order where automated information factories churn out new products and deliver them in new ways.

Core markets for printing and publishing will remain substantially intact into the 21st century. While the quantity of commercial printing and publishing may gradually level over the next decade, the quality of demand will change rapidly. Networked interactive media and information will grow rapidly over the next five years, but measured by advertising revenues, digital media will still be less than 10% of print media. Most categories of printing and publishing now have print, digital media, networked printing, and networked interactive product alternatives.

The most important change is not the displacement of print to non-print media, but the evolution of printing and publishing processes from craft-based manufacturing to computer- and communications-based services. New categories of demand are emerging as key attributes of printing and publishing products are redefined. The dynamic of market demand is about new ways to reach the right person, with the right content, at the right time, in the right place, in the right form for intended uses.

Metaphors for printing and publishing workflows include "the market of one", "just in time printing and publishing", "mass-customization of media", "on-demand" and "1-to-1 communications." To address emerging market requirements, printing and publishing workflows will need a higher metabolism in order to be more responsive to customers, with failsafe quality, faster, more flexible, just-in-time delivery, with the capability of handling an increasing volume of smaller transactions profitably. Printing and publishing processes must and will be reengineered to provide the level of performance required by new categories of demand as measured by cost, quality, service, speed, and flexibility.

Changing Business Conditions

The printing and publishing business environment is changing. An emerging digital economy is restructuring the industry as well as transforming relationships both within and between customers, service providers and suppliers. The need for rapid innovation and rapid response to changing markets are facts of business life. The emerging digital infrastructure will propel inter-business communication, workflow, and content management to new levels of performance, flexibility, and service. The business of printing and publishing wants to be real-time, with zero lag time between identification and fulfillment of need. Advantage will go to companies that, together with their customers, providers and suppliers, move information better and respond more quickly to changing market needs than their competition.

The need for more rapid response to changing markets, better service, higher quality, lower costs, and greater flexibility are driving businesses in the printing and publishing industry to restructure and to reinvent the way they do business. To drive out costs and reduce processing latency, industries and businesses must take steps to compress their value chain.

Cross-industry mergers and acquisitions by news, periodical, book, entertainment, broadcast, and cable companies will be a fact of life into the new millennia. Communications media are repositioning, seeking to leverage their costs of content and distribution across multiple media via the emerging digital infostructure. Looking at the technology base we find infostructure misalignment, contrasting computing architectures, competing standards, and conflicts between legacy systems and the new technologies.

Networked Digital Workflows

The focus is on process reengineering to achieve rapid response, short cycle time, quality failsafing, on-line customer service, low transaction costs, low materials usage, minimum inventory costs, and minimum distribution costs. Networked digital workflows introduce new forms of printing and publishing, conducting all business over inter/intranets, establishing print networks for distributed printing, publishing and document management services, and supporting both "push" and "pull" demand models.

Content can be either "pushed" or "pulled" through the network from databases. High-performance networked systems with links to databases make variable page, personalized, and custom content an option. Through printing networks, the distribute-and-print model emerges as an alternative to print-and-distribute. Internetworking business enables lean, flexible printing and publishing with just-in-time, on-demand delivery. As customer, provider, and suppliers internetwork and make information and systems interoperable, they can molecularize to achieve minimum inventories and processing costs, as well as more rapid response to changing market conditions.

Specific networked workflows will vary depending on the type of business, its markets, technology base, the roles it chooses to play in the networked digital process. Networked digital workflows support a richer and more coordination-intensive infor-

Dynamics of Market demand
- *right person: generalized, customized, personalized*
- *right content: text, graphics, images, sound, video*
- *right time: fixed vs. continuous delivery*
- *right place: centralized, regionalized, localized*
- *right form: print, multimedia, Web-based*

- *Print—print and distribute—an old model slowly changing.*

- *Digital media—replicate and distribute—like print, only send a disk.*

- *Networked print—distribute and print—lots of potential with new digital printers.*

- *Networked digital media—display and transact—the Web-based model.*

mation logistics in which content, workflow, and business information streams are fully integrated. Digitization begins sooner in the process, ends later, and encompasses more of the total communication and information flow between businesses than has ever been possible with analog or digital-analog workflows. All business-to-business communication and as much work-in-process as possible is handled across networks.

Customers can inquire through the 'net, learn how to prepare jobs, obtain estimates, submit work, determine status, and conduct business transactions. Workflow quality failsafing begins by aligning processes across the value flow to head off problems, by communicating preliminary specifications and to all affected parties before ever producing the job. Prepress services, printers, binderies, and fulfillment services, for example, could simulate the job, suggest alternatives to customers, estimate and quote production, provide job-specific instructions, plug-ins, color profiles, business forms and applets to handle preflight at the customer site. Before transmitting a job (such as a digital advertisement) the source files could be prechecked to ensure not only that the PDF would process correctly, but also that content elements had been made to the correct specifications for the application, medium, and reproduction process.

Networked digital content creation adds digital photography to the repertoire of digital-analog techniques. All input capture devices will evolve into color-managed network appliances. As the price performance of desktop tools to manipulate image and graphic content and master pages continues to improve, new levels of capability emerge for feature-based content editing, cross-media authoring and meta-design, and variable and custom data merge, to name a few. Many applications will be re-engineered to function as software objects across inter/intranet front-ends.

Prepress, printing, and post-press functions will become increasingly automated processes across networks. Incoming work will be digitally logged into content, workflow, and business transaction databases, triggering credit checks, content file preflighting, scheduling and resource allocation. Digital job specifications will provide the information needed to program individual prepress, press, and post-press operations. Networked digital process steps will be threaded, multi-tasked, or concurrently executed as needed, with status updates posted to a common database visible to everyone concerned. Even off-line functions will be coordinated digitally.

One of the hallmarks of networked digital workflows will be color-managed digital printing, proofing and remote proofing. The defining application will be digital advertising in newspapers, magazines and catalogs. Pigment-based inkjet printing may provide a near-term breakthrough towards direct proofing on actual stock with colorants that behave like inks on press. Prep will move from files, imagesetters and imposetters towards databases; variable and custom data merge; and computer-to-film, computer-to-plate, and computer-to-press. The benefits of moving to an integrated content, workflow and business database are major, impacting operations up-stream as well as down-stream. The benefits of computer-to . . . are basically incremental and depend on successful front-end integration of the digital workflow that feeds the prep-step.

Network digital workflows leverage all kinds of printing output—analog sheet-fed, web offset, gravure and flexo presses, and hybrid presses as well digital ones. Specifications have been developed for digitally-driven press rooms and digitally coordinated binderies. These workflows enable multiple distribute-and-print and on-demand printing models as well as print-and-distribute. Networked digital workflow management is based on new control structures. Digital insourcing and outsourcing is common place. Functions are performed in a natural order wherever it makes most sense. Integration across multiple businesses is achieved through open network infrastructure standards, shared process semantics, application-level content specifications, standard file and database formats, and industry standards for electronic data interchange. Distributive workflows are coordinated through network communications to common (synchronized) databases containing evolving content and product information, workflow schedule and current job status, business relationship and financial data, and management information.

Quality control is achieved through industry-standard network-based color management that features immediate access to current device and process profiles, local calibration measurements. Digital files replace analog materials as links between some steps, eliminating some materials usage and facilitating correction cycles.

Networked digital content management involves file formats, standard page description languages, and digital archives with dedicated librarian applications to index, search and retrieve data. Multipurposing requires maintaining multiple versions of source content. Networked digital business systems are fully integrated with work-in-process and content management. Electronic data interchange and, in some instances, electronic commerce are standard operating procedure.

Quantum improvements in printing and publishing workflow are possible by combining principles of business process reengineering with architectures for distributive workflow, integrated business systems, and media-independent content management.

The PDF is unique in that it is both the product and the enabler of this new world order. As a product it is the view file delivered on disk or over the Web. The information consumer receives their content in a format-rich form where type and image are miraculously preserved.

As an enabler, the PDF is the raw material of new workflows that re-engineer the way we print or present. In the history of human communication there has never been a method that could be so totally re-purposed, re-used, re-played, and even regurgitated on demand.

CHAPTER

THE IDEAL DIGITAL DOCUMENT

This is our opinion chapter. It's not as far out as blue sky and not as close as down-to-earth. Let's start by saying that TIFF/IT and other bitmap files are just a dumb buckets of bits. They cannot help you re-purpose information into other media. They cannot help you drive different output devices from the same data. They cannot get you on the Web. They can be archived but there isn't much you can do with them when they come out of hibernation—especially if you have changed output devices in the meantime. They cannot be read on different platforms—or even any platform. They are just a dumb buckets of bits. WYGI-WYD—what you get is what you deserve.

Some commercial printers like bitmap files because they see them as the digital equivalent of film—unchanging, unchangeable. But they will soon find that the world of information dissemination is fickle. It wants what it wants when it wants it. That means it may want print today and electronic publishing tomorrow. It may want to proof on one device now and a remote proofer later. It may print on an inkjet machine today and an offset press next week. Bitmap workflows were a reaction to the eccentricities of PostScript. They were a good idea at the time but now there is an alternative.

Who owns TIFF?
TIFF was developed by Aldus and Microsoft Corp, and the specification was owned by Aldus, which merged with Adobe Systems, Incorporated. Consequently, Adobe Systems may hold the copyright for the TIFF specification. TIFF is a trademark, formerly registered to Aldus, and which is probably claimed by Adobe but is not listed on their Web trademark page. The TIFF/IT-P# is a standard and we have never seen a copyright indicated.

A common complaint of TIFF is rooted in its flexibility. For example the TIFF format permits both MSB ("Motorola") and LSB ("Intel") byte order data to be stored, with a header item indicating which order is used.

There are old, poorly written TIFF programs on the PC and assume that all TIFF files are Intel byte order. It is easy to write a TIFF-writer, but very difficult to write a fully TIFF-compliant reader.

TIFF uses 4-byte integer file offsets to store image data, but a TIFF file cannot have more than 4 gigabytes of raster data (and some files have begun to approach this boundary). However, this is 4 GB of compressed data, and so if the compression ratio is high enough, theoretically a TIFF image could be much larger.

PDFs are smart files. They carry each element—text, images—as both a separate and an integrated unit. You can keep the file intact or break it apart. You can set and then re-set color management information. You can read it and print it anywhere at almost any time. Only PDFs meet the demands for CD-ROM (and DVD-ROM), Web and print publishing. PDFs and PDF workflows are the future of printing and publishing.

PostScript—The Almost Standard

The world of digital prepress and digital printing exists because of PostScript. Although it is the "standard" for driving almost every high-end printing device, it has never been a standard standard. It is a de facto standard, which means that everyone uses it as a standard but no one want to admit it is a standard.

The PDF takes PostScript to a higher level. It removes the variability. It virtually pre-RIPs the document to speed its progress through the workflow. Supra is an architecture with a lot of little RIPs distributed throughout the system. It divides and conquers. Think of Supra and such systems as a hydra, the mythological creature with seven heads. By the way, it had one main head as well.

Now, add in the functionality of trapping and imposition and OPI and hot folders and more—the PDF-based workflow that Agfa is assembling as an example—and you have one of the most efficient methods for moving jobs around an electronic system.

The Present

This book was our attempt to centralize much of our research about the Acrobat PDF in one place at one time. We have provided tips and tricks on how it works and how you can apply it for high-end printing. A smattering of information on RIPs and systems and workflows has been included because the PDF does not stand alone. It is a part of a system, a piece of the whole.

There is still a lot to come. Plug-ins will proliferate. New systems will evolve. Functionality will improve. Hopefully this book will provide the foundation for your use of the PDF and an understanding of its place in the digital printing world of today and tomorrow.

The Future
There are lots of ideas in the printing and publishing industries about how work will flow through automated systems.

• CIP3 stands for Consortium International Prepress, Press and Postpress and it is being developed by the Fraunhofer Institute for Computer Graphics in Darmstadt, Germany, with a number of industry suppliers involved. The goal is to link the prepress, press and postpress parts of the process into one cohesive system. Where does PDF fit in? Plug in! We think you will see plug-ins for many special purposes and the links between all print-related functions makes sense.

• Magazines and newspapers will finally get digital ads. Some might be bitmaps until the comfort level with PDF grows. DDAP will go PDF as ad agencies discover its power and pre-press services discover the many new value-added services they can provide. Like converting the print version of an ad to a Web version. OK, the format and size might be a problem. But new conversion programs might convert the ad into something more appropriate for the Web.

PDF is cross platform compatible—MS-DOS, Mac OS, Windows and UNIX. Outline font information is embedded within the document, potentially resolving font problems. PostScript files can be distilled to PDF and PDF files can be previewed on a monitor for verification prior to printing. However, until the 3.0 version of Acrobat was announced on June 3, 1996, there were several major limitations to Adobe Acrobat:
• It was incapable of handling CMYK data.
• Incompatibility with OPI precluded workflows employing high-resolution images.
• Printing attributes, color management data, and resolution were not be included in the file.
• Embedded EPS files created unworkable situations.
Now digital ads are a reality.

The CIP3 group has released version 2.0 of its Print Production Format (PPF) description for the standardization of communicating digital data between prepress, press and postpress (finishing) equipment. Version 2.0 includes several additions and improvements, a result of continued dialogue between the CIP3 members and the information obtained from beta sites of CIP3 users. The main differences between version 1.0 and 2.0 are in the areas of compression techniques available for images, used to generate ink setting information, and more detailed descriptions on how PostScript is used. For the postpress or finishing data generation the folding information has been positioned in a separate structure providing more direct access.

Version 2.0 specifications of the CIP3 PPF are available from Fraunhofer-IGD at http://www.igd.fhg.de/www/igd-a1/cip3.

Currently the members of CIP3 are: Adobe, Agfa, Barco, Creo, Crosfield, Ekotrading-Inkflow, Eltromat Polygraph, Ewert Ahrensburg Electronic, Goebel, Harlequin, Heidelberg, Koenig & Bauer - Albert, Kolbus, Komori, Linotype-Hell, MAN-Roland, Mitsubishi Heavy Industries, Müller Martini, Polar Mohr, Scitex, Screen, Ultimate, Wohlenberg

Problems with digital ads

Inadequate instructions	51%
No proof	44%
Unspecified fonts	38%
Non-printable fonts	19%
Unspecified file types or software version	37%
Missing images	36%
Proof not latest version	31%
Improper bleeds	35%
Improper page size	32%
Unspecified embedded graphics	31%
Incorrect trapping	19%
Proof not a verifiable color proof	18%
Unspecified Color	16%

These limitations are addressed in Acrobat 3.0. Magazines could be in a position to accept PDF files for computer-to-plate technology very soon. With such a file format standard in place the next step will be to build a series of recommendations/specifications for the submission of ads, including instructions, media, resolution, fonts, colors, page sizes and bleeds.

Future Speculations

- Color management will become a no-brainer. Color management is like the weather; everyone talks about it but no one has really done anything about it. There are partial solutions out there but they are just 10-foot logs trying to ford a 12-foot stream.

- Acrobat will not be the only PDF kid on the block anymore. Third-party vendors will create PDF writers, readers, editors and printers. Remember, Acrobat is only the interface, not the format. So, from now on say a PDF file, not an Acrobat file.

- CGATS will continue to push TIFF/IT as a standard and perhaps it will play some role in the future. A walk-on.

- Within a few years there may not be PostScript as we know it—only PDF.

- Where functions are performed in future workflows may not be an issue. OPI, trapping, imposition and other functions can be done before the RIP, in the RIP, or beyond the RIP. The RIP will be just another function in an automated workflow. The RIP-centric world will change to a PDF-centric world.

- "Computer-to" approaches will continue to accelerate, mandating new workflows that automate individual processes. In the printing plant of the past people spent a lot of time carrying things around—disks, films, plates, proofs, job folders and more. In the printing plant of the future the only carrying-on will be over a cable. Or maybe in the lunch room.

- PDF editing applications will abound. Because of PDF's object-oriented structure, you will be able to move objects (text, images, line art) around the page like a page layout application. You will be able to open a PDF file and move the objects on the page. So, when the client says, "Can you move that up a smidge?", you can.

- Standards will continue to evolve. There may always be a disparity between what the standards groups create and what the industry actually uses. Our problem has not been that we do not have standards; our problem is that we have too many of them.

- The operative word may be "remote." Creative professionals will send view files to clients; clients will send annotated files back. Final documents will be sent to graphic services; remote proofing data will be sent back. The graphic arts firm of the future will be a wired wonder.

- It's the PDF, stupid. By now you are getting tired of the term. And our comments about it. But keep in mind that it only takes one technology to make an industry. The lowly PDF will re-vitalize print by making it easier for people to get to print. And beyond.

Merging several sources of information to a single PDF file

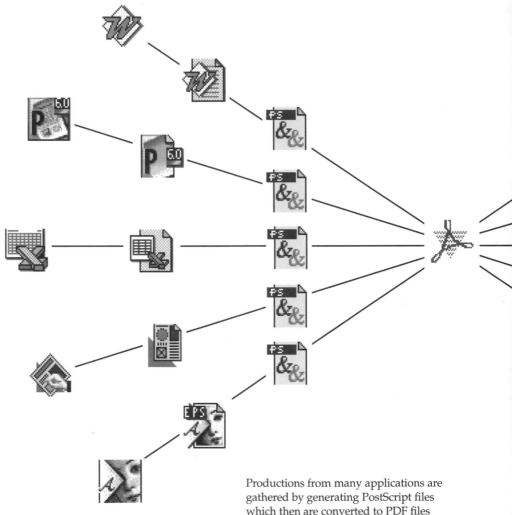

Productions from many applications are gathered by generating PostScript files which then are converted to PDF files with Distiller.

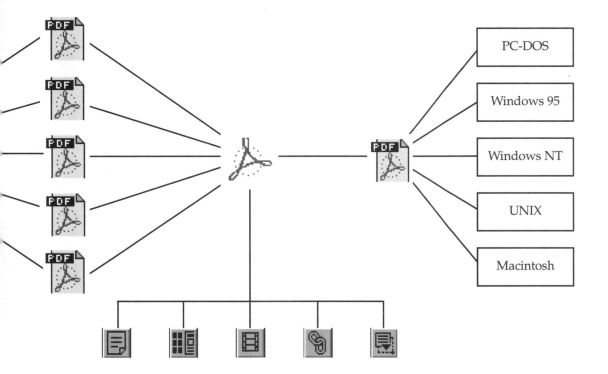

The individual PDF files are opened in Acrobat Exchange or similar PDF editing application. Here the files can be merged in to a single file. QuickTime movies, sound, forms and linking is done to produce a single device independent file that includes all information.

PDF: The Next Generation of Publishing Workflows

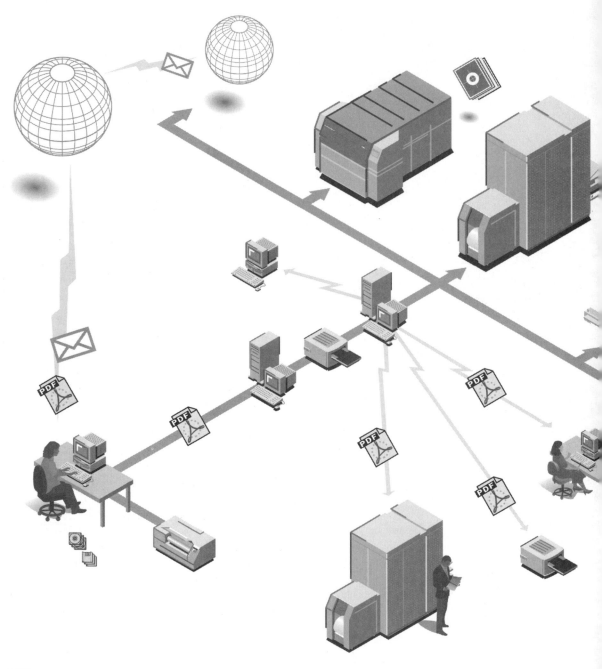

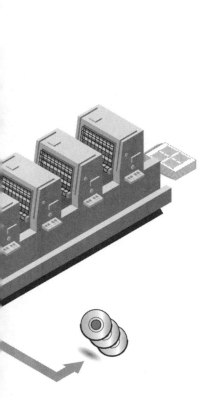

Device independence

The need for printing drivers or printer description files has made printing more device-dependent than users would have liked. But now the Acrobat 3.0 PDF provides the best method yet for storing and defining a document for print. The same file can be used for digital proofing, imposed film imagesetting, computer-to-plate, black and white document printer, color printer/color press, Web viewable and printable documents, and archivable formats.

Media independence

Use the medium that best suits your message: page or imposed film, imposed plate—polyester or aluminum, digital color proof, demand printing from digital printers and presses, Web files, CD-ROM files, or digital image archives. Publishing has never had more opportunity for extending its franchise and re-inventing itself.

PDF publishing

Publish in print or non-print form. For instance, convert a year's worth of your publication to PDFs and record them on a CD-ROM. Sell this reference archive at a value-added price. Why? It's not just the publication, you can also search through all issues to find the keywords and information you want. Users will pay a premium for search and retrieval. You can also put the PDFs on the Web with a password and give it only to paid subscribers. Create an archive of issues from past years. PDFs retain the look and feel of your publication. Users can read them on-screen or print them out on almost any PostScript printer.

Distributed printing and remote proofing

Send PDFs with the efficacy of electronic communication to additional print sites to bring reproduction closer to the point of distribution . . . with the assurance that each site will print a uniform and predictable document. Send PDFs back to the client to proof on a digital proofer with proper color transforms. PDFs speed the production process . . . and also speed the delivery process.

Afterword

I develop relationships with vendors who may use products to enable transfer of data to and from that vendors products. For example, I spend a lot of my energy developing things like remote proofing strategies, with our goal to make it as bulletproof as faxing a document. Without a standard file format, it will be chaos. In my view, Adobe has provided us with a way to fully descibe a color document using the PDF file structure which can, at this writing, permit us to view on screen and print documents as the creator of that document intended. More importantly, we can do this without making the file as difficult to edit as a raster only page description. If you are confused about this, try correcting the spelling of a name on a bitmap image of a fax in Photoshop. This is where we are the high-end color prepress industry today.

Indeed, some of us send QuarkXPress documents, others PostScript, as "print to disk" files, some send proprietary Scitex CT and LW files; many believe that raster files such as TIFF/IT (similar in concept to sending bitmapped fax data) may be the most reliable method. This hodgepodge of file structures and stategies often requires that the recieving end of the file do things, sometimes heroic things, to simply view the file, never mind actually print out the file. As there are no free Macintosh or Wintel client applications that can even view a TIFF/IT file, I see the TIFF/IT file structure as the format of choice when I want to have an unscreened digital version of four-color file, just prior to imaging it onto some high-resolution media such as film or plates. Otherwise, PDF can do the job.

What the PDF file format promises is a future where we can perform a blind transfer. As an industry, we need a way to eliminate the ambiguity of exchanging color pages. We need a way for the creator, author or originator of a color document to transfer that document while carrying all the elements and entities that are required for that document to achieve the intended results at the receiver's end, without heroic intervention at that receiver's site; in essence, we need to accomplish a reliable exchange of graphical color data between the sender and the receiver.

When I discusssed this concept with Jim Meehan, one of the authors of the PDF specifications at Adobe, I asked him pointedly (as I think many of us would have) what the main differences were between PostScript and PDF, and why I should be confident in PDF as a file structure that will lend itself to blind transfers of color documents. What he explained was so elegant, I simply had to give him credit for it, lest you think I was so clever; he explained to me that that a PostScript file is a "program," an actual application that is created, sent and then run inside the PostScript RIP, and that a PDF file is more of an "object database." When a PostScript file (or PostScript application, more accurately) is run, the PostScript commands are interpreted and then rasterized into a bitmap and normally imaged to paper, film or plates. The objects that describe graphical elements and entities in PostScript are difficult to parse or otherwise find or extract. This is where we are today with PostScript. Moreover, If you want to make a simple edit, such as a spelling correction, you normally need to go back to the original application file that created it. Editing PostScript is not very straightforward. In the case of PDF, this simply is not the case. Using Adobe applications such as Exchange, one can make that spelling correction on all the popular computer platforms and, if Distiller were set up properly, without requiring you to have the fonts!

In my view, this is the very first file format that actually resolves the main problems we encounter in our industry's current prepress workflow. It is compact enough to transmit efficiently, can be created, opened, viewed, and edited without depending on a specific computer platform and, in the case of simply viewing and printing, can be accomplished using an application that can be downloaded for free from Adobe's Web site (www.adobe.com). Any advertising agency, design firm, prepress service provider, publisher, or printing company can prove this to themselves by aquiring the free Adobe Acrobat reader and then downloading the facing page. Go to http://www.tool.net/friends/jahn/pdf3/cmyk.pdf, and you can view and print this document (it is under 600 K) without a hitch. Go ahead. Open it and print it. If you have any problems, E-mail me at mikejahn@jahn.com. I am confident that you will be suprised to learn just how easy it works.

Michael Jahn

cmyk.pdf

To download this PDF version 1.2 test file (it is about 500k), go to:

http://www.tool.net/friends/jahn/pdf3/cmyk.pdf

R	G	B	C	M	Y	K	CMY
		100		100		100	100
		90		90		90	90
		80		80		80	80
		70		70		70	70
		60		60		60	60
		55		55		55	55
		50		50		50	50
		45		45		45	45
		40		40		40	40
		35		35		35	35
		30		30		30	30
		25		25		25	25
		20		20		20	20
		15		15		15	15
		10		10		10	10
		07		07		07	7
		05		05		05	5
		04		04		04	4
		03		03		03	3
		02		02		02	2
		01		01		01	1

This PDF document contains all fonts and is in cmyk colorspace. The full document size (or MediaBox) is 9.5 x 12 inches, with each side cropped 0.5 of an inch, so the CropBox is 8.5 x 11. This permits the file to display in Adobe Acrobat Reader™ as was intended, with trim marks and register marks hidden.

Should you desire to print the document with the trim marks and register marks, open this PDF file in Adobe Acrobat Exchange™ and go to the Document menu, select Crop Pages from the menu and make all margins zero.

The above Screen snips show how Acrobat Distiller™ version 3.0 was set up when we distilled the Quark XPress™ generated PostScript.

Special thanks to Internet Tool & Die for hosting the site at www.tool.net. I used the 4-Sight PPP™ application that is included with 4-Sight ISDN Manager™ to dial into the internet via ISDN and upload this file via FTP to the URL listed above.

You will need the free Adobe Acrobat™ Reader application to view this document. Go to http://www.adobe.com/prodindex/acrobat/readstep.html to download it.

This document and pdf file was created & designed by Michael Jahn, OEM Manager, 4-Sight L.C. It may be distributed without permission.

Questions? Contact: Michael Jahn via email at michael_jahn@4sight.com • 800 West Cummings Park, Suite 3700 • Woburn, MA • 01801 • 888.247.4448 ext 116

Index